LEE COUNTY
KENTUCKY

Births, Deaths and Marriages

1874–1878 and
1900–1910

Margaret Millar Hayes

HERITAGE BOOKS
2013

HERITAGE BOOKS
AN IMPRINT OF HERITAGE BOOKS, INC.

Books, CDs, and more—Worldwide

For our listing of thousands of titles see our website
at
www.HeritageBooks.com

Published 2013 by
HERITAGE BOOKS, INC.
Publishing Division
100 Railroad Ave. #104
Westminster, Maryland 21157

Other Heritage Books by the author:

Lee County, Kentucky 1880 Annotated Census, Including the 1880 Mortality Schedule
Lee County, Kentucky Births, Deaths, and Marriages, 1874–1878 and 1900–1910
Owsley County, Kentucky 1880 Annotated Census (Revised)
Reconstructed Marriage Records of Breathitt County, Kentucky, 1839–1873
Reconstructed Marriage Records of Owsley County, Kentucky, 1843–1910: Part 1 (A–L)

International Standard Book Numbers
Paperbound: 978-1-55613-661-0
Clothbound: 978-0-7884-6905-3

PREFACE

Lee County, Kentucky was formed in 1870 from Breathitt, Estill, Owsley, and Wolfe Counties. Present day Lee County is surrounded by the counties of Breathitt, Owsley, Jackson, Estill, Powell, and Wolfe.

The records contained in this book were taken from microfilmed copies of the records filed with the state of Kentucky during the period 1874-1878 and 1900-1910.

Birth records are set up as follows:
name of child, date of birth (sex, color, born alive or dead, place of birth)
name of father & mother;
birthplace of father & mother;
residence of parents; remarks

Death records are set up as follows:
name (sex, color, marital status; age; occupation) date of death, cause of death; birthplace; residence; place of death; names of parents; birthplace of father & mother; remarks
Age at death is in years, unless otherwise stated.

Marriage records are set up as follows:
name of GROOM (residence, age, marital status, occupation, birthplace of groom) names or birthplaces of parents
BRIDE (residence, age, marital status, birthplace of bride)
names or birthplaces of parents
date & place of marriage; remarks

NOTES:

The counties listed in each entry are in Kentucky, unless otherwise noted. Thus, "Lee" denotes Lee Co., KY. When it is "Lee Co., VA" it will be so stated.

Anything in brackets [--] has been added by me for the sake of clarification or as an annotation.

Words in quotation marks are spelled as is, such as "soar" throat, instead of sore throat.

Causes of death:

Carbuncle = painful, localized, pus-bearing inflammation of the tissue beneath the skin, more severe than a boil, and having several openings.

Colic = acute abdonimal pain caused by various abnormal conditions in the bowels

Consumption = a disease that causes part of the body to waste away, especially tuberculosis of the lungs.

Croup = inflammation of the respiratory passages, with labored breathing, hoarse coughing, and spasms of the larynx.

Dropsy = abnormal accumulations of serous fluid in cavities or tissues of the body.

Gravel = kidney stones or stones in the bladder.

Infantine = infantile or childlike

Intemperance = excessive drinking of alcoholic liquor.

Pulmonary consumption = wasting away of the lungs.

Quinsy = inflammation of the tonsils, accompanied by the formation of pus.

Scrofula = tuberculosis of the lymphatic glands, especially of the neck, characterized by the enlargement and degeneration of the glands.

Typhoid fever = of or like typhus

Typhus fever = infectious disease transmitted to man by the bite of fleas, lice, etc.; characterized by fever, nervous disorder, weakness, and an eruption of red spots on the skin.

iv

Abbreviations used:

@ = at	aff. = affidavit
a/L = also listed	al. = alive
appar. = apparently	b. = born
Blk = black	c = circa (about)
ch/o = child of	Clk = Clerk's
Co. = County	Cr. = Creek
d. = died	da = days
d/o = daughter of	F = female
fem = female	inc. = included
M = male	md = married
mgs. = marriages	mo = months
Mul. = mulatto	nn = not named
par. = parents	poss. = possibly
R. = residence	remd. = remarried
S = single	s/b = should be
s/o = son of	uk = unknown
W = white	w/with
wd = widowed	wf/o = wife of
yr. = years	------- = left blank
------? = unreadable	

County, City, etc. abbreviations:

Beattyvl = Beattyville	
Belle Pt. = Belle Point	
Boonevl = Booneville	
Bourb = Bourbon Co.	Br. = Breathitt Co.
Breck = Breckinridge	Clk = Clark Co.
Earnestv = Earnestville	
East Bernstet = E.Bernstet	
Est. = Estill Co.	Fay = Fayette Co.
Germ. = Germany	Hanc. = Hancock Co.
Harl. = Harlan Co.	Ire. = Ireland
Jack. = Jackson Co.	Jeff = Jefferson Co.
Jess. = Jessamine	John. = Johnson Co.
Let. = Letcher Co.	Lex. = Lexington
Linc = Lincoln Co.	Louisvl = Louisville
Mad. = Madison Co.	Mag. = Magoffin Co.
Menf = Menifee Co.	Montg. = Montgomery
Morg = Morgan Co.	Ows. = Owsley Co.
Pend = Pendleton Co.	Per = Perry Co.
Pow. = Powell Co.	Pul. = Pulaski Co.
Rockc = Rockcastle	Taz. = Tazewell
Wash = Washington Co.	Wlf = Wolfe Co.

Occupation abbreviations:
B'smth = Blacksmith
crptr. = carpenter
frm = farmer/farming
Hkpr. = housekeeper/keeping house
Hwf. = housewife
Ins.Agt. = Insurance Agent
lab. = laborer
Lum.Insp. = lumber inspector
mcht. = merchant
mech. = mechanic
Mine Op. = mine operator
pub.wks. = public works
RR = Railroader
sch.tchr. = school teacher
Steno = stenographer
Tel.Op = Telegraph Operator

Sources for information in brackets:
BOws. = Births Owsley Co., KY [RMT]
RCB = Records of Carole Bays
RFR = Records of Floyd J. Ratz
RJB = Records of James F. Bowman, decd.
RMT = Records of Marge Turner
RWO = Records of William O'Connor

Name abbreviations:
Alex. = Alexander
Benj. = Benjamin
Chas. = Charles
Eliz. = Elizabeth
Jno. = Jonathan
Margt. = Margaret
Saml. = Samuel
Wm. = William

Archd. = Archibald
Cath. = Catherine
Edw. = Edward
Geo. = George
Jos. = Joseph
Robt. = Robert
Thos. = Thomas

BIRTHS.

Date of Birth	Name of Child	Sex	Born alive or dead	Place of Birth	Name of Father of Child	Maiden Name of Mother of Child	Color (white, black or mulatto)
June 28th 1874	John McVay	Male	Alive	Co. C. Ky.	Harrison McVay	Bets Madison	Black
July 20th 1874	George Rodgers	"	"	Harrison Co. Ky.	Wilson Rodgers	Harriet Stafford	White
July 10 1874	Louis McClintey	"	"	Carter Ky.	John H. Colyer	Amanda Wilkins	"
1874	William Bowers	Female	"	"	Juh H. Bowers	Maggie E. Harte	"
September 4, 1874	Nancy Bruington	White	Alive	Carter Ky.	James Elizabeth Bruington	Amanda Burch	"
August 1874	"	Female	dead	Carter Ky.	Minor Eta	Martin Harrison	"
April 20 1874	William G. Asbery	Male	Alive	"	Richard Bennett	Ages Burton	"
October 16th 1874	Samuel McCabe	"	"	"	John B. Asbery	James Colyer	"
January 14 1874		Female	dead	"	James McCabe	Lucy Burnett	"
February 1874	Iowa Asbery	"	Alive	"	Trelining Burnett	Agnes Burton	"
April 25 1874	Willie McVay	Male	"	"	George Delaney	Melinda O. Blount	"
February 1874	Margaret Allcott	Female	"	"	Harley Roy	Minerva Wilson	"
March 28th 1874	Mary E. Allcott	"	"	"	William Allcott	Hannah Wilson	"
August 1874	Anna Grundy	Male	"	"	William O. Webb	Escretia Steward	"
Sept 1874	Walter Grundy	"	"	"	Baby Bruington	Margetta Bryant	"
" 1874	Howard Boldin	"	"	"	Ada L. Grady	Harriet Yorkinson	"
May 14 1874	Mirtie Amelda	"	"	"	James O. Phillips	Mary J. McGuire	"
March 1st 1874	William Delaney	Male	"	"	Virgil Howard	Mary Burrus	"
July 10 1874				"	William Delaney	Luisella A. Eata	"
" 1874	Carter B. Steward		Male	"	Mark F. Curry	Mary Norman	"
June 17 1874	Felix Smith	Female	"	"	Mc Smith	Sophia Brandenburgh	"
1874		Male	"	"	William Burnett	Harry Plummer	"
January 15 1874	Richard Riggs	"	"	"	Andrew Riggs	Nancy Smith	"
August 28 1874	Rose B. Smith	"	"	"	John W. Smith		"
Dec 25 1874	Alonzo Martin	Female	"	"	John Shetson		"
March 24 1874	Alfred Yorth	Male	"	"	William Yorth	Martha Ann Hamilton	"
Feb 5 1874	Pierce Steward	Female	"	"	Robert Steward (Tenant)	Ella Fitzhue	"
Dec 24 1874	Lucy Steward	"	"	"		Ondy A. McKenzie	"
April 5 1874	Emerine McThomas	"	"	"	William Thomas	Grant McEnroe	"
August 1874	Nettie Roman	"	"	"	Elias McMasters	Mary Underwood	"
January 24 1874	Luther Brushie	"	"	"	William R. Brushie	John R. Matlin	"
May 13 1874	Mary E. Houston	Male	dead	"	Wm. W. Houston	Belle Morrijio	"
June 17 1874				"	William A. Wright	Louisa Brown	"

BIRTH RECORDS - 1874-1878

NOTE: There were no births listed for the year 1877.

ABNER
Phebe E., 17 April, 1876 (F W alive Lee)
    d/o Louis Abner & Amelia Ann Gum
    par. b. Ows. & Est.; R.Lee [see deaths]
ADAMS
Nanie B., 1 Feb., 1875 (F W alive Est.)
    d/o Randall Adams & Mary J. Baker
    par. b. Let. & Ows.; R.Lee
AKERS
Alice E., 16 April, 1876 (F W alive Lee)
    d/o Stephen D. Akers & Rhoda Jameson
    par. b. Ows. & Est.; R.Lee
Laura B., 18 July, 1878 (F W alive Lee)
    d/o Stephen D Akers & Rhoda Akers [Jameson]
    par. b. Ows. & Est.; R.Lee
ALDER
Harvey, 29 May, 1878 (M W alive Lee)
    s/o Wm. Alder & Susan Cornelius
    par. b. Powell Co., VA & Clay; R.Lee
ANGELL
Amos, 10 March, 1874 (M W alive Lee)
    s/o Henderson Angell & Rebeca Steel
    par. b. Ows. & Floyd; R.Lee
William J., 1 Dec., 1874 (M W alive Lee)
    s/o Wilburn Angell & Zerilda Mays
    par. b. Ows. & Br.; R.Lee
    [Wilburn & "Merilda" md. 25 Dec., 1853 Br.]

1

ARNOLD

Lorenzo D., 19 Feb., 1876 (M W alive Lee)
    s/o Geo. W. Arnold & Mary Thomas [see mgs.]
    par. b. PA & Ows.; R.Lee
Lydia T., 8 Dec., 1876 (F W alive Lee)
    d/o Newton J. Arnold & Sallie Riley
    par. b. Lee Co., VA & Fay.; R.Lee
Minie, 14 Nov., 1874 (F W alive Lee)
    d/o Geo. W. Arnold & Mary Thomas
    par. b. Lee Co, VA & Ows.; R.Lee
Phillip, 19 Feb., 1878 (M W alive Lee)
    s/o James Arnold & Arminta Stamper
    par. b. Lee Co, VA & Morg; R.Lee
Sarah A, 12 March, 1875 (F W al. Hanc. Co, TN)
    d/o Wm. D. Arnold & Lucy A. Fairchilds
    par. b. Lee Co, VA & Hanc. Co, TN; R.Lee
Zachary, 5 May, 1876 (M W alive Lee)
    s/o James Arnold & Arminta Stamper
    par. b. Lee Co, VA & Morg; R.Lee

ARROWOOD

Jesse, 17 March, 1878 (M W alive Lee)
    s/o Wm. J. Arrowood & Sarah Turner
    par. b. Clark & Br.; R.Lee
    [Wm. Jasper & Sarah md. c1865 Br.]

ASBERRY

Wm. G., 16 Oct., 1874 (M W alive Lee)
    s/o John C. Asberry & Nancy Coffer
    par.b. Taz. Co, VA & Montg. Co, VA; R.Lee

ASBILL

Robert C., 14 April, 1875 (M W alive Lee)
    s/o Samuel B. Asbill & Mary E. Gourley
    par. b. Ows. & Carter Co, TN; R.Lee

ASHCRAFT

Algernon, 24 Dec., 1874 (M W alive Lee)
    s/o Wm. Ashcraft & Hannah Wilson [see mgs.]
    par.b. Ows & Lee Co, VA; R.Lee [see deaths]
Minnie, 26 Jan., 1875 (F W alive Lee)
    d/o Wm. Ashcraft & Hannah J. Wilson
    par. b. Ows. & Lee Co, VA; R.Lee
    [NOTE: Algernon & Minnie's birthdates are
    too close. The 1880 census lists her as
    age 4, which would make her b. 1876.]
Ruth, 22 Oct., 1875 (F W alive Lee)
    d/o John Ashcraft & Mary J. Shearer
    par. b. Ows. & Ows. Co., VA [s/b KY]; R.Lee
    [John & Mary md. 4 Oct., 1871 Lee]

BALDWIN
----, 4 Aug., 1876 (M W alive Lee)
   s/o Wm. J. Baldwin & Celia Johnson
   par. b. KY & NC; R.Lee
BARKER
Mary J., 24 April, 1876 (F W alive Lee)
   d/o John Barker & Sabina Bryant
   par. b. Est. & KY; R.Lee
   [John & Sabina md. 9 May, 1872, Lee]
Rachel M., 1 Aug., 1878 (F W alive Lee)
   d/o John "Baker" & "Sifa" Bryant
   par. b. Est. & Morg.; R.Lee
BARRETT
Clarinda, 7 Nov., 1876 (F W alive Lee)
   d/o Harison Barrett & Vicy Couch
   par. b. Br. & Br.; R.Lee
Rosa Ann, 27 Dec., 1874 (F W alive Lee)
   d/o "Varrison" Barrett & Visa "Crouch"
   par. b. Ows. & Ows.; R.Lee
   [NOTE: listed as Rebecca in deaths]
BEACH
Mary P., 9 June, 1876 (F W alive Lee)
   d/o Clifton M. Beach & Lizzie Crawford [see
   mgs.]; par. b. Kanawha [Co.], WV & Ows.;
   R.Lee
BEATTY
Baxter, 25 Aug., 1878 (M W alive Lee)
   s/o Milo Beatty & Fanny Sewell
   par. b. Br. & Br.; R.Lee
   [Milo & Fanny md. 17 Oct., 1872, Lee]
Edmond A., 15 March, 1875 (M W alive Lee)
   s/o Milo Beatty & Fannie Sewell
   par. b. Ows. & Br.; R.Lee
---- [Lena], 14 March, 1875 (F W alive Lee)
   d/o James M. Beatty & Carline McGuire
   par. b. Franklin Co., MO & Ows.; R.Lee
   [see deaths for Caroline McGuire Beatty]
BEGLEY
----, 16 May, 1875 (- W dead Lee)
   ch/o G. D. Begley & Rachel Davidson
   par. b. Clay & Clay; R.Lee
Caly, 21 Dec., 1878 (F W alive Lee)
   d/o John Begley & Mary Warren
   par. b. Per. & Harl.; R.Lee

3

BEGLEY (cont.)
Hettie, 16 Dec., 1876 (F W alive Lee)
    d/o Swempfield Begley & Mary Davidson
    par. b. Per. & Clay; R.Lee
John, 10 July, 1878 (M W alive Lee)
    s/o Elisha H. Begley & Margaret Davidson
    par. b. Per. & Br.; R.Lee
BELCHER
Elizabeth, 28 May, 1878 (F W alive Lee)
    d/o Manson Belcher & Anna Spencer
    par. b. Per. & Ows.; R.Lee
BELLAMY
Sarah V., 1 April, 1878 (F W alive Lee)
    d/o Wm. M. Bellamy & Cath. France
    par. b. Scott Co., VA & Scott Co., VA;
    R.Lee
BENNETT
-----, 20 March, 1874 (F W dead Lee)
    d/o Richard Bennett & Agnes Burton
    par. b. Est. & Est.; R.Lee [listed twice]
-----, 25 Sept., 1878 (M W dead Lee)
    s/o Richard Bennett & Agnes Burten
    par. b. Est. & Est.; R.Lee
nn, --------- 1875 (F? W dead Lee)
    ch/o Richard Bennett & Agnes Burton
    par. b. Est. & Est.; R.Lee
---- [Belinda], - Jan., 1874 (F W alive Lee)
    d/o Wm. Bennett & Nancy Pitman
    par. b. Est. & Ows.; R.Lee
Esbella, 14 Feb., 1878 (F W alive Lee)
    d/o John Bennett & Susan Burten
    par. b. Est. & Est.; R.Lee
Richard(?), 6 March, 1875 (M W alive Lee)
    s/o John Bennett & Susannah Bennett
    par. b. Est. & Est.; R.Lee
BESS
Geo. W., 29 Dec., 1875 (M W alive Lee)
    s/o John Bess & Kizah Hughes
    par. b. Est. & Est.; R.Lee
BOWLIN
Callie, 24 Jan., 1874 (F W alive Lee)
    d/o Wm. P. Bowlin & Sarah Martin
    par. b. Henry Co, VA & Scott Co, VA; R.Lee
BOWMAN
Alexander, 27 Nov(?), 1874 (M W alive Lee)
    s/o Green Bowman & Eliz. Jones
    par. b. Ows. & Ows.; R.Lee

4

BOWMAN (cont.)

Anna, 20 July, 1876 (F W alive Lee)
    d/o Weslie Bowman & Eliz. Mills
    par. b. Est. & Est.; R.Lee
    [John Wesley & Eliz. md. Sept., 1854 Br.]
Arminta, 20 Dec., 1878 (F W alive Br.)
    d/o John W[esley] Bowman & Eliz. Mills
    par. b. Est. & Est.; R.Fay.
Lucy C. [Lizzie], 18 May, 1874 (F W alive Lee)
    d/o Andrew J. Bowman & Nancy J. Evans
    par. b. Br. & Br.; R.Lee
    [Andrew Jackson & Nancy Jane md. 1862 Br.]

BOYD

Samuel, 22 April, [1878] (M Blk alive Lee)
    s/o Peter Boyd & Polly Banner
    par. b. --- & Mad.; R.Lee

BRANDENBURGH

nn, 4 March, 1874 (M W alive Lee)
    s/o Wm. Brandenburgh & Almeda Winkle
    par. b. Ows. & Est.; R.Lee
Andrew, - Sept., 1875 (M W alive Lee)
    s/o Wm. Brandenburgh & Amelia Winkle
    par. b. Ows. & Est.; R.Lee
Catherine, 28 Aug., 1875 (F W alive Lee)
    d/o Hardin Brandenburgh & Martha Spivy
    par. b. Est. & Johnson Co, TN; R.Lee
Daniel G., 6 Jan., 1875 (M W alive Lee)
    s/o Thos. Brandenburgh & Nancy A. Thomas
    par. b. Est. & Ows.; R.Lee
James C., 5 April, 1874 (M W alive Lee)
    s/o Jas. P. Brandenburgh & Mary A. Day
    par. b. Ows. & Claiborne Co, TN; R.Lee
John C., 14 April, 1878 (M W alive Lee)
    s/o Jackson Brandenburgh & Mandy Arnold
    par. b. Est. & Lee Co, VA; R.Lee
Kenez, 23 June, 1874 (M W alive Lee)
    s/o Jas. H. Brandenburgh & Mary Thomas
    par. b. Est. & Clay; R.Lee
Lucy A., 29 May, 1874 (F W alive Lee)
    d/o Joel Brandenburgh & Sarah Plummer
    par. b. Ows. & Br.; R.Lee
Margret, 14 June, 1876 (F W alive Lee)
    d/o Saml. J. Brandenburg & Eliz. Gilespee
    par. b. Ows. & Ows.; R.Lee
    [Saml. & Eliz. md. 9 Sept., 1875 Lee]

BRANDENBURGH (cont.)
Margaret, 27 Aug., 1878 (F W alive Lee)
    d/o George H. Brandenburgh & Eveline
    Brandenburgh; par. b. Ows. & Ows.; R.Lee
    [Geo. & Eveline md. 1 Feb., 1873 Lee]
Mary E., 6 April, 1874 (F W alive Lee)
    d/o Saml. D. Brandenburgh & Lucy A. Hoover
    par. b. Est. & Lee Co, VA; R.Lee
BROWN
Susan A., 20 Dec., 1878 (F Blk alive Lee)
    d/o James Brown & Lourena Maddox [see mgs.]
    par. b. Nelson & Ows.; R.Lee
BRYANT
Sena Lena E., 18 Aug., 1876 (F W alive Lee)
    d/o James F. Bryant & Anna Stephens
    par. b. Knox & Whitley; R.Lee
BURCHEM
Martha A., 28 Oct., 1878 (F W alive Lee)
    d/o James Burchem & Levisa Fletcher
    par. b. Logan Co, VA & Mag.; R.Lee
    [listed twice, same date, but w/par. b.
    Taz. Co., VA & Floyd on 2nd one]
BURKE
Effa D., 26 July, 1878 (F W alive Lee)
    d/o Geo. P. Burke & Vivia McGuire [see mgs]
    par. b. Daviess & Lee; R.Lee
BURKHART
Elizabeth, 10 May, 1878 (F W alive Br.)
    d/o Isaac Burkhart & Nancy J. Fletcher
    par. b. Harl. & Mag.; R.Lee

CABLE
Ettoffa, 14 Oct., 1878 (F W alive Lee)
    d/o Millard Cable & Sarah Hobbs
    par. b. Ows. & Wlf.; R.Lee
    [she appar. d. before the 1880 census]
CASITY
Edmond, 10 June, 1874 (M W alive Lee)
    s/o David J. Casity & Mary Norman
    par. b. Morg. & Ows.; R.Lee
    [David & Mary Ann md. 1856/7 Br.]
CENTERS
Rachel M., 28 Nov, 1878 (F W alive Montg.)
    d/o Stephen Centers & America Rose
    par. b. Morg. & Ows.; R.Montg.
    [Stephen & America md. 8 March, 1871 Lee]

6

CHAMBERS
Joseph, 7 July, 1875 (M W alive Lee)
    s/o John R. Chambers & Marium Bowman
    par. b. Morg. & Est.; R.Lee
    [John Rose & Mariam md. 29 July, 1850 Br.]
CHILSON
Lucy B., 6 July, 1876 (F W alive Lee)
    d/o Albert Chilson & Margret Tincher
    par. b. Stuben Co., NY & Ows.; R.Lee
    [Albert & Margaret md. 1 Oct, 1875 Lee]
CLAY
John W., 25 June, 1874 (M Blk alive Lee)
    s/o Henry Clay & Bell Maddox
    par. b. Oldham & Ows.; R.Lee
COCKERHAM/COCKRAM
Dora A., 31 Aug., 1878 (F W alive Lee)
    d/o Zachariah T. Cockram & Margaret A Lutes
    par. b. Wlf. & Ows.; R.Lee
Margaret J., 26 Sept, 1878 (F W alive Lee)
    d/o --------- & Lydia A. "Keene"
    par. b. -- & Br.; R.Lee
    [Martin Cockram & Lydia A. King md. 9 June,
    1858 Br.; Lydia listed as Divorced 1880]
Orlena, 7 Dec., 1876 (F W alive Lee)
    d/o Martin Cockerham & Lydda A. King
    par. b. Br. & Br.; R.Lee
COLE
Charles H., 14 Jan., 1875 (M W alive Lee)
    s/o Birdine B. Cole & Nancy A. Crawford
    par. b. Est. & Br.; R.Lee
Felix D., 10 April, 1874 (M W alive Lee)
    s/o Speed S. Cole & America Snodgrass
    par. b. Ows. & Wash. Co, VA; R.Lee
Nettie, 9 April, 1876 (F W alive Lee)
    d/o Speed C. Cole & "Armina" Snodgrass
    par. b. Ows. & Wash. Co, VA; R.Lee
Robert G., 4 Oct., 1878 (M W alive Lee)
    s/o Speed C. Cole & America G. Snodgrass
    par. b. Est. & Wash. Co, "KY"; R.Lee
Zilla, 22 March, 1878 (F W alive Lee)
    d/o Wm. H. Cole & Nannie E. Steel
    par. b. Ows. & Ows.; R.Lee
COLLINS
nn, - Jan., 1875 (M W dead Lee)
    s/o Howard Collins & Nancy Dunigan
    par. b. Clay & Lee Co., VA; R.Lee

COLLINS (cont.)
Polly Ann, 11 Sept., 1878 (F W alive Lee)
    d/o Howard Collins & Nancy Dunigan
    par. b. Clay & Lee Co, VA; R.Lee
COMBS
Kenneth B., 20 April, 1875 (M W alive Lee)
    s/o Tinsley Combs & Sarah E. Goosey
    par. b. Ows. & Ows.; R.Lee
Mary, 20 March, 1874 (F W alive Lee)
    d/o ------- & Margaret Combs
    par. b. --- & Per.; R.Lee; illegitimate
Pely, 28 Jan., 1878 (M W alive Lee)
    s/o Joseph Combs & Eliza Farmer
    par. b. Br. & Harl.; R.Lee
Williamette, 26 Dec., 1876 (F W alive Lee)
    d/o T[insley] L. Combs & Sarah E. Goosey
    par. b. Ows. & Ows.; R.Lee
CONGLETON
Ada, 30 May, 1878 (F W alive Lee)
    d/o Isaac Congleton & Paulina Asbell
    par. b. Ows. & Ows.; R.Lee [see deaths]
Lilly A., 11 Jan., 1876 (F W alive Lee)
    d/o Isaac G. Congleton & Polina Asbill
    par. b. Ows. & Ows.; R.Lee
COOMER
-----, 24 Dec., 1876 (M W dead Lee)
    s/o Henry Coomer & Eliz. Vanderpool
    par. b. Lee Co, VA & Ows.; R.Lee
Benjamin, 12 Dec., 1878 (M W alive Lee)
    s/o David Coomer & Nancy Lucas
    par. b. Lee Co, VA & Lee Co, VA; R.Lee
    [David & Nancy md. 17 July, 1871 Lee]
James, 5 April, 1875 (M W alive Lee)
    s/o Henry Coomer & Eliz. Vanderpool
    par. b. Lee Co, VA & Ows.; R.Lee
Jesse G., 19 Jan., 1876 (M W alive Lee)
    s/o Leander Coomer & Eleanor Marshall
    par. b. Adair & Stokes Co, NC; R.Lee
Mary B., 27 Aug., 1876 (F W alive Lee)
    d/o Riley Coomer & Lourana Coomer [Kilburn]
    [see mgs.]; par. b. Est. & Br.; R.Lee
Nannie E., 3 April, 1876 (F W alive Lee)
    d/o Patton Coomer & Emeline Smith
    par. b. Lee Co., VA & Br.; R.Lee
Sarah A., 23 March, 1874 (F W alive Lee)
    d/o Tyler Coomer & Martha Wells
    par. b. Lee Co, VA & Lee Co, VA; R.Lee

8

COOMER (cont.)
Susan M., 24 June, 1876 (F W alive Lee)
    d/o Jackson Coomer & Louisa Coomer
    par. b. Lee Co, VA & Lee Co, VA; R.Lee
COUCH
Barny, 18 Nov., 1876 (M W alive Lee)
    s/o Henry Couch & Anna Marshall
    par. b. Br. & Lee Co., VA; R.Lee
Henry, 5 June, 1878 (M W alive Lee)
    s/o Henry Couch & Anna Marshall
    par. b. Clay & Lee Co, VA; R.Lee
CRABTREE
Elisabeth, 5 Oct., 1875 (F W alive Lee)
    d/o Geo. A. Crabtree & Eliza Rogers
    par. b. Lee Co, VA & Est.; R.Lee
Horace J., 17 Dec., 1875 (M W alive Lee)
    s/o Elkana Crabtree & Malissa Combs
    par. b. Est. & Morg.; R.Lee
    [Elkana & Malissa md. 13 Mar, 1875 Lee]
Mary L., 30 Sept., 1875 (F W alive Lee)
    d/o David S. Crabtree & Eliz. R. Wilson
    par. b. Lee Co, VA & Lee Co, VA; R.Lee
CRAWFORD
Cally H., 22 Oct., 1878 (F W alive Lee)
    d/o James Crawford & America Plummer
    par. b. Br. & Br.; R.Lee
Cynthia Ann, - Dec., 1874 (F Mul alive Lee)
    d/o Jefferson HAMPTON & Hanah Crawford
    par. b. Ows. & Br.; R.Lee; illegitimate
Dilla A., 13 April, 1875 (F W alive Lee)
    d/o Marcus Crawford & Litha Fowler
    par. b. Ows. & Est.; R.Lee [see deaths]
George W., 29 June, 1878 (M W alive Lee)
    s/o Elihu Crawford & Eliz. Sparks
    par. b. Est. & Est.; R.Lee
Nancy Bell, 24 May, 1878 (F W alive Br.)
    d/o D[aniel] B. Crawford & Armilda Lawson
    par. b. Br. & Morg.; R.Br.
    [Daniel Boone & Armilda md. 1873 Morg.]
Susan, 19 Sept., 1874 (F W alive Lee)
    d/o James Crawford & America Plummer
    par. b. Br. & Br.; R.Lee [see deaths]
CREECH
Floyd, 3 March, 1875 (M W alive Lee)
    s/o Dewitt C. Creech & Matilda Spencer
    par. b. Lee Co, VA & Ows.; R.Lee

CRITZER
Idama [Ida Mae], 22 April, 1878 (F W al. Lee)
    d/o Leander Critzer & Almeda "Pitt"
    par. b. Nelson Co., VA & Montg.; R.Lee
---- [Margaret], 27 Sept, 1876 (F W alive Lee)
    d/o Leander Critzer & Almelia "Frazier"
    par. b. Loudon Co, VA & Montg.; R.Lee
CROACH/CROOCK(?)
Nancy, 4 Dec., 1878 (F W alive Lee)
    d/o Sylvester Croach(?) & Nancy Ann Horn
    par. b. Est. & Est.; R.Lee
CROOK
Charles W. D., 17 Feb, 1878 (M W alive Lee)
    s/o Mathew Crook & Catharine Flannery
    par. b. Grayson Co., VA & Scott Co., VA;
    R.Lee
Wm., 26 Oct., 1875 (M W alive Lee)
    s/o Mathew U. Crook & Catharine Flanary
    par. b. Br. & Scott Co., VA; R.Lee
CUNDIFF
Nancy, 9 May, 1878 (F W alive Lee)
    d/o Robert Cundiff & Mary J. Wyatt
    par. b. Br. & Wlf.; R.Lee
    [Robt. & Mary Jane md. 26 July, 1877 Br.]
CURRY
Eliza E., 8 Feb., 1878 (F W alive Lee)
    d/o James M. Curry & Louvin[a] J. Smyth
    par. b. Est. & Est.; R.Lee
    [twin of George E.]
    [James & Louvina md. 30 March, 1871, Lee]
George E., 9 Feb., 1878 (F W alive Lee)
    d/o James M. Curry & Louvina J. Smith
    par. b. Est. & Est.; R.Lee
    [twin of Eliza E.]
James B., 5 Nov., 1876 (M W alive Lee)
    s/o Geo. D. Curry & Eliza Combs
    par. b. Lee Co., VA & Br.; R.Lee
    [Geo. & Eliza md. 26 April, 1872 Lee]
Margaret A., 1 Nov., 1878 (F W alive Lee)
    d/o Geo. D. Curry & Eliza J. Combs
    par. b. Lee Co., VA & Br.; R.Lee

DAMRELL/DAMERIL
Elizabeth, 10 Oct., 1878 (F W alive Lee)
    d/o Joel Damrell & Phoebe Wright
    par. b. Lee & Let.; R.Lee

DAMRELL/DAMERIL (cont.)
Josephine, 20 May, 1876 (F W alive Lee)
    d/o Joel Damrell & Pheba Wright
    par. b. Br. & Let.; R.Lee
Lucinda, 19 Oct., 1875 (F W alive Lee)
    d/o John Dameril & Eliz. A. Angel
    par. b. Br. & Ows.; R.Lee
DANIEL
Albert F., 16 May, 1875 (M W alive Lee)
    s/o Scott Daniel & Matilda Robinson
    par. b. Ows. & Ows.; R.Lee
Alfred, 15 July, 1875 (M W alive Lee)
    s/o Wm. Daniel & Susan Brandenburgh
    par. b. Br. & Ows.; R.Lee
DAVIS
nn, 12 Dec., 1875 (M W alive Lee)
    s/o James "H" Davis & Georgiann Duff
    par. b. Ows. & Lee Co, VA; R.Lee
    [appar. d. before the 1880 census]
Julia, 1 Aug., 1878 (F W alive Lee)
    d/o James "L" Davis & George Ann Duff
    par. b. Ows. & Glascow, MO; R.Lee
    [mother George Ann d. 11 days later]
nn [Nannie], 1 June, 1874 (F W alive Lee)
    d/o Orlando Davis & Demaris McGuire
    par. b. Ows. & Ows.; R.Lee
    [Orlando & Demmy md 17 April, 1873 Lee]
DAY
Green B., 29 Jan., 1875 (M W alive Lee)
    s/o Ira Day & ---------- [Eliza]
    par. b. Lee Co., VA & Harl.; R.Lee
Willie, 11 Jan., 1874 (M W alive Lee)
    s/o Newbery Day & Diana Day
    par. b. Lee Co., VA & Est. Co, VA [KY];
    R.Lee
DEATON
Fanny, 14 Feb., 1876 (F W alive Lee)
    d/o Alfred Deaton & Alwilda King [see mgs.]
    par. b. Br. & Br.; R.Lee
George, 22 Dec., 1874 (M W alive Lee)
    s/o Dison Deaton & Polly Hensley
    par. b. Br. & Wash. Co, PA; R.Lee
    [Dison & Polly md. 1862/3 Br.]

DEATON (cont.)
James K. P., 27 Sept., 1875 (M W alive Lee)
    s/o John Deaton & Rebecca Lucas
    par. b. Mathew Co, IN & Lee Co, VA; R.Lee
    [NOTE: There is a Matthews, IN in Grant Co,
    but no Mathew Co., IN] [d. April, 1880]
    [John & Rebecca md. 1849/50 Br.]
Sarah C., 14 Feb., 1878 (F W alive Lee)
    d/o Alfred Deaton & Almilda King
    par. b. Br. & Wlf.; R.Lee
DITMAN
Sallie A., 1 May, 1876 (F W alive Lee)
    d/o Jesse Ditman & Polly Estes
    par. b. Ows. & Ows.; R.Lee
DOUGHERTY
Henry, 24 May, 1875 (M W alive Lee)
    s/o Francis Dougherty & Martitia Cole
    par. b. Donnegal Co., Ire. & Ows.; R.Lee
DUNAGAN/DUNAGIN
Berry R., - May, 1876 (M W alive Lee)
    s/o Berry Dunagin & Martisha Bryant
    par. b. Lee Co., VA & Br.; R.Lee
Charles, 31 Jan., 1874 (M W alive Lee)
    s/o James E. Dunagan & Amanda Spence[r]
    par. b. Ows. & Lee Co, VA; R.Lee
Jesse G., 30 July, 1874 (M W alive Lee)
    s/o Berry Dunagan & Matilda Bryant
    par. b. Lee Co., VA & Br.; R.Lee
Nancy, 4 Sept., 1874 (F W alive Lee)
    d/o Wm. Dunagan & America Couch
    par. b. Lee Co., VA & Br.; R.Lee
Zura E., 13 March, 1878 (F W alive Lee)
    d/o James E[wing] Dunigan & Amanda Spencer
    par. b. Ows. & Pul.; R.Lee
DUNAWAY
Charley, 12 Feb., 1878 (M W alive Lee)
    s/o Wm. Dunaway & Quintilla Estes
    par. b. Ows. & Est; R.Lee
    [Wm. & Quintilla md. 15 Dec., 1870 Lee]
Mazilla, 21 June, 1875 (F W alive Lee)
    d/o Wm. Dunaway & Quintilla A. Estes
    par. b. Ows. & Est; R.Lee
Thomas, 16 April, 1876 (M W alive Lee)
    s/o Thomas Dunaway & Eliz. Dunagin
    par. b. Est. & Lee Co, VA; R.Lee
    [see deaths for par. Thos. & Eliz.]

12

DUNAWAY (cont.)
Wm., 10 March, 1874 (M W alive Lee)
   s/o Wm. Dunaway & Quintilla A. Estes
   par. b. Ows. & Est; R.Lee [see deaths]
DURBIN
Demia, 25 March, 1874 (F W alive Lee)
   d/o John Durbin & Malinda Hamilton
   par. b. Est. & Est.; R.Lee
   [John & Malinda md. 13 Feb, 1874 Lee;
   Demia listed as age 5 in 1880 census]
Edward, 28 Oct., 1875 (M W alive Lee)
   s/o Joseph Durbin & Mary C. Reynolds
   par. b. Ows. & Est.; R.Lee
   [Jos. & Mary md. 4 Oct., 1871 Lee]
Lucyan, 15 Oct., 1878 ("M" W alive Lee)
   d/o Josiah Durbin & Evoline Warner
   par. b. Ows. & Ows.; R.Lee
Marion L., 4 Dec., 1875 (M W alive Lee)
   s/o Marion Durbin & Eliz. Newton
   par. b. Ows. & Ows.; R.Lee
   [Marion & Eliz. md. 13 April, 1871 Lee]
Minna A., 27 April, 1878 (F W alive Lee)
   d/o Ambrose Durbin & Rebecca Wells
   par. b. Est. & VA; R.Lee
   [Ambrose & Rebecca md 21 Mar, 1872 Lee]
Wm. D., 19 March, 1876 (M W alive Lee)
   s/o Wm. F. Durbin & Emeline Plowman
   par. b. Est. & Est.; R.Lee
   [Wm. & Emeline md. 21 Oct., 1872 Lee]

EDENS
John M., 10 July, 1874 (M W alive Lee)
   s/o John W. Edens & Amanda Walton
   par. b. Est. & Est.; R.Lee
   [John & Amanda md. 1 June, 1870 Lee]
ESTES
-----, - Aug., 1874 (M W dead Lee)
   s/o Mason Estes & Martha Newman
   par. b. Ows. & Ows.; R.Lee
Clarinda, 24 March, 1876 (F W alive Lee)
   d/o Asberry Estes & Abba [Ibby] Newton
   par. b. Est. & Est.; R.Lee
Emily, 31 Jan., 1878 (F W alive Lee)
   d/o Mason Estes & "Mashel" [Martha] Newman
   par. b. Ows. & Ows.; R.Lee

ESTES (cont.)
Jacob, 23 Feb., 1878 (M W alive Lee)
    s/o Hiram Estes & Nancy Newton
    par. b. Ows. & Ows.; R.Lee
Mary E., 5 Oct., 1878 (F W alive Lee)
    d/o Henry Estes & Margaret A. Newman [see
    mgs.]; par. b. Est. & Ows.; R.Lee
Sarah J., 16 Oct., 1875 (F W alive Lee)
    d/o Mason Estes & Martha Newman
    par. b. Ows. & Ows.; R.Lee
EVANS
-----, 27 Nov., 1876 (M W alive Lee)
    s/o Huram Evans & Isabell Arnold
    par. b. Ows. & Hanc. Co, TN; R.Lee
Martha, 23 April, 1876 (F W alive Lee)
    d/o Jesse Evans & Eliz. Gordon
    par. b. Ows. & Smith Co, VA; R.Lee
EVE
Anna R., - May, 1876 (F W alive Lee)
    d/o Wm. B. Eve & Sally F. Smith
    par. b. Boone & Ows.; R.Lee

FARLER
Martha J., 8 Dec., 1875 (F W alive Lee)
    d/o John Farler & Mary Howell
    par. b. Per. & IN; R.Lee
FARMER
Silas, 19 Feb., 1874 (M W alive Lee)
    s/o John F. Farmer & Margaret J. Gray
    par. b. Ows. & Ows.; R.Lee
    [John & Margaret md. 27 March, 1873 Lee]
FIELDS
Benjamin F., 3 March, 1878 (M W alive Ows.)
    s/o Hiram Fields & Polly Fields
    par. b. Per. & Per.; R.Lee
David B., 4 April, 1875 (M W alive Lee)
    s/o Harrison Fields & Josephine Robinson
    par. b. Logan Co., VA & Clay; R.Lee
FIKE
Lee [Leander], 29 April, 1876 (M W alive Lee)
    s/o Joseph Fike & Lucinda Burns(?) [see
    mgs.]; par. b. Ows. & Clay; R.Lee
FLETCHER
Shelba, 10 July, 1878 (M W alive Lee)
    s/o Merida Fletcher & Eliza Buckhart
    par. b. Mag. & Hardin; R.Br.
    [Merida & Eliza md. 9 July, 1877 Br.]

14

FRAILEY/FRALEY
-----, 11 June, 1874 (F W dead Lee)
    d/o Henry Fraley & "Lou Ellen" Gum
    par. b. Ows. & Ows.; R.Lee
    [Henry & Susan E md. 3 March, 1871 Lee]
B. Delli, 21 Nov., 1878 (M W alive Lee)
    s/o James Frailey & Violet Fletcher
    par. b. Br. & Br.; R.Lee
    [B. Delli & Butler D. poss. same person]
    [James & Violet md. 9 July, 1877 Br.]
Benj. T., 4 Jan., 1874 (M W alive Lee)
    s/o Stephen Fraley & Helen France
    par. b. Ows. & Scott Co, VA; R.Lee
    [Stephen & Helen md. 28 Aug., 1873 Lee]
Butler D., 21 Nov., 1878 (M W alive Lee)
    s/o James Frailey & Violet Fletcher
    par. b. Br. & Br.; R.Lee
    [B. Delli & Butler D. poss. same person]
Lucinda, 29 March, 1876 (F W alive Lee)
    d/o Henry Frailey & Susan E. Gum
    par. b. Est. & Ows.; R.Lee
Stephen, 18 May, 1878 (M W alive Lee)
    s/o Henry Frailey & Susan E. Gum
    par. b. Ows. & Ows.; R.Lee
FRANCE
Josephine, 2 June, 1878 (F W alive Lee)
    d/o Lewis France & Geniva Bowman
    par. b. Scott Co, VA & Ows; R.Lee
FULKS
Juletta, 12 Nov., 1875 (F W alive Lee)
    d/o Henry Fulks & Nancy G. Palmer
    par. b. Ows. & Br.; R.Lee
    [Henry & Nancy md. 27 March, 1873 Lee]
Wm. S., 18 Jan., 1874 (M W alive Lee)
    s/o Henry Fulks & Nancy G. Palmer
    par. b. Ows. & Br.; R.Lee

GABBARD
Rachel, 30 May, 1875 (F W alive Lee)
    d/o Claiborne Gabbard & Mary Chambers
    par. b. Clay & Morg.; R.Lee
    [Claiborne & Mary md. c1864 Br.]
GENTRY
Diademia, 14 Feb., 1875 (F W alive Lee)
    d/o Joseph K. Gentry & Mariam Kincaid
    par. b. Lee & Ows.; R.Lee
    [Jos. & Mariam md. 26 Oct., 1871 Lee]

GILBERT

Martha, 7 March, 1876 (F W alive Park Co, IN)
    d/o John Gilbert & Eliz. Willis
    par. b. Ows. & Clay; R.Lee
    [John & Eliz. md. 23 May, 1871 Lee]

GILLESPIE

Hiram F., 17 Nov., 1875 (M W alive Lee)
    s/o Wm. R. Gillespie & Susan Wright
    par. b. Est. & Morg.; R.Lee

GOE

Arthur, 22 Dec., 1878 (M W alive Lee)
    s/o Benj. T. Goe & Mary F. Howard
    par. b. Clark & Est.; R.Lee

Phillip, 15 Feb., 1875 (M W alive Lee)
    s/o Benj. T. Goe & Mary F. Howard
    par. b. Clark & Ows.; R.Lee
    [he appar. d. before the 1880 census]

GOOSEY

Josephine, 6 June, 1875 (F W alive Lee)
    d/o David Goosey & Armina Roach
    par. b. Est. & Ows.; R.Lee

Manda, 27 July, 1878 (F W alive Lee)
    d/o David Goosey & Armina Roach
    par. b. Clay & Est.; R.Lee

GOURLEY

Walter, 24 May, 1874 (M W alive Lee)
    s/o John C. Gourley & Hanah Tomlinson
    par. b. Carter Co, TN & Wash. Co, VA; R.Lee

GRAY

Harden, - Jan., 1876 (M W alive Lee)
    s/o Wm. Gray & Mary Rader
    par. b. Ows. & Ows.; R.Lee

Lucy, 27 Feb., 1875 (F W alive Lee)
    d/o John M. Gray & Ellen Newton
    par. b. Ows. & Ows.; R.Lee
    [John & Ellen md. 1 Sept., 1870 Lee]

Robert A., 14 April, 1878 (M W alive Lee)
    s/o Wm. Gray & Mary J. Raider
    par. b. Ows. & Ows.; R.Lee

GRIFFIN

Benj., 2 May, 1875 (M W alive Lee)
    s/o Jesse Griffin & Mary Lynch
    par. b. Mad. & Est.; R.Lee

Bitha J., 20 June, 1878 (F W alive Lee)
    d/o Charles Griffin & Ara Ingram
    par. b. Mad. & Est.; R.Lee

16

GRIFFIN (cont.)
Rosanna E., 1 Dec., 1875 (F W alive Lee)
    d/o Charles Griffin & "Mary" Ingram
    par. b. Mad. & Est.; R.Lee
GUM
Kitsey [Catharine], 16 Dec, 1875 (F W al. Lee)
    d/o Stephen Gum & Eliz. Maloney
    par. b. Est. & Br.; R.Lee

HALE
James W., 9 April, 1874 (M W dead Lee)
    s/o Wm. Hale & Mary Jane Hoover
    par. b. Russell Co, VA & Lee Co, VA; R.Lee
HALEY
Abba, 3 March, 1878 (F Blk alive Lee)
    d/o Austin Haley & Mary Maden [Maddox] [see
    mgs]; par. b. Est. & Rowan; R.Lee
Frank, 12 Feb., 1876 (M Mul alive Lee)
    s/o Austin Haley & Mary Maddox
    par. b. Ows. & Ows.; R.Lee; "These are
    colored folks"
HALL
Cordelia, 4 Oct., 1878 (F W alive Lee)
    d/o John C. Hall & Lucy Ann Tincher [see
    mgs.]; par. b. Ows. & Ows.; R.Lee
    [apparently twin of Joseph]
Joseph B., 4 Oct., 1878 (M W alive Lee)
    s/o John C. Hall & Lucy Ann Tincher
    par. b. Ows. & Ows.; R.Lee
    [apparently twin of Cordelia]
Mary E., 7 Oct., 1875 (F W alive Lee)
    d/o Joseph Hall & Mary Thomas
    par. b. Ows. & Clay; R.Lee
Permelia, 22 March, 1875 (F W alive Lee)
    d/o Harvey Hall Jr. & Sarah Thomas
    par. b. Ows. & Ows.; R.Lee [see deaths]
    [Harvey & Sarah md. 19 Sept., 1872 Lee]
HAMILTON
Lucy A., 9 Oct., 1876 (F W alive Lee)
    d/o John S. Hamilton & Martha Isaacs
    par. b. Ows. & Ows.; R.Lee
HAMMAN
Oma R., 6 Dec., 1875 (M W alive Lee)
    d/o John Hamman & Eliz. A. McGuire
    par. b. Montg. & Est.; R.Lee

HAMMAN (cont.)
Robert B., 12 Nov., 1876 (M W alive Lee)
    s/o Phillip Hamman & Phebe J. Stamper [see
    mgs.]; par. b. Montg. & Ows.; R.Lee
Thomas G., 26 Jan., 1878 (M W alive Lee)
    s/o John Hamman & Eliz. McGuire
    par. b. Montg. & Est.; R.Lee
HAMPTON
Lucy, 22 Aug., 1878 (F Blk alive Lee)
    d/o Jefferson Hampton & Violet Herald
    par. b. KY & Br.; R.Lee
    [Jefferson & Violet md. 13 March, 1875 Br.]
Malissa, 17 June, 1875 (F Blk alive Lee)
    d/o Wilson Hampton & Mary J. Crawford
    par. b. Ows. & Br.; R.Lee
Martha J., 4 March, 1876 (F Mul. alive Lee)
    d/o Saml. Hampton & Avary Crawford
    par. b. Johnson Co, TN & Br.; R.Lee; "These
    are colored folks"
HARRIS
William, ----- 1874 (M W alive Lee)
    s/o John R. Harris & Maggie C. Ward
    par. b. Charlotte Co., VA & VA; R.Lee
    [John & Maggie md. 24 June, 1873 Lee]
HATTON
Armina, 28 May, 1876 (F W alive Mad.)
    d/o Wm. S. Hatton & Jane Smith
    par. b. Est. & Br.; R.Lee
    [Wm. & Jane md. 14 Aug., 1875, Br.]
Mary E., 14 Dec., 1876 (F W alive Lee)
    d/o Wm. J. Hatton & Eliza J. Maloney
    par. b. Br. & Br.; R.Lee
HIERONYMOUS
Cordy, 16 July, 1876 (F W alive Lee)
    d/o Thos. Hieronymous & Tandy M[argt.] Bush
    par. b. Est. & Est.; R.Lee
HILL
Abba, 4 Dec., 1878 (F W alive Lee)
    d/o John [Joel in 1880] Hill & Arrena Moore
    par. b. NC & NC; R.Lee [twin of Pal.]
Pal. [Pallo Allo], 7 Dec, 1878 (F W alive Lee)
    d/o John [Joel in 1880] Hill & Arrena Moore
    par. b. NC & NC; R.Lee [twin of Abba]
Samuel J., 2 Jan., 1875 (M W alive Lee)
    s/o James A. Hill & Anna F. Beatty
    par. b. Sims "Co.", NC & Franklin Co., MO;
    R.Lee [NOTE: Sims, NC is in Wilson Co, NC]

HILL (cont.)
Wm. H., 2 Aug., 1875 (M W alive Lee)
    s/o Robt. C. Hill & Mary J. Cockrell
    par. b. Br. & Br.; R.Lee
HOBBS
Cora, 23 May, 1875 (F W alive Lee)
    d/o Wm. Z. Hobbs & Sarah Shoemaker
    par. b. Lee Co., VA & Ows.; R.Lee
Mary Ann, 20 Dec., 1878 (F W alive Lee)
    d/o Wm. Z. Hobbs & Sarah J. Shoemaker
    par. b. Lee Co., VA & Wlf.; R.Lee
HOLLAND
Archd., 27 Feb., 1874 (M Mul. alive Lee)
    s/o Tarlton Holland & Chaney Hampton
    par. b. Br. & Let.; R.Lee
Malissa, 16 Sept., 1875 (F Mul. alive Lee)
    d/o Tarlton Holland & "Clarsa" Hampton
    par. b. Let. & Morg.; R.Lee
    [see deaths for mother Chaney]
HORN
Sidey G., 8 March, 1878 (M W alive Lee)
    s/o John Horn & Nancy Durbin;
    par. b. Est. & Est.; R.Lee
HOWELL
nn [Decatur], 26 Dec., 1875 (M W alive Lee)
    s/o Elias Howell & "Leonia" Newman
    par. b. Est. & Ows.; R.Lee
nn [Mary], 1 Sept., 1876 (F W alive Lee)
    d/o Samuel P. Howell & Eliza J. Tincher
    par. b. Est. & Est.; R.Lee
Simpson, 19 Dec., 1875 (M W alive Lee)
    s/o unknown & Eveline Howell
    par. b. Ows. & Ows.; R.Lee; illegitimate
Wm. J., 19 Aug., 1878 (M W alive Lee)
    s/o Elias T. Howell & Leanah Newman
    par. b. Est. & Ows.; R.Lee
HOWERTON
Chas. H., 15 Sept., 1878 (M W alive Lee)
    s/o John W. Howerton & Bell Menefee
    par. b. Morg. & Bourbon; R.Lee
Mary E., 13 May, 1874 (F W alive Lee)
    d/o John W. Howerton & Bell Menifee
    par. b. Morg. & Bourbon; R.Lee
Nancy, 29 Oct., 1878 (F W alive Lee)
    d/o Albert G. Howerton & Augusta Berger
    [see mgs.]; par. b. Morg. & IN; R.Lee

HURLEY
Mahaley, 30 June, 1876 (F W alive Lee)
    d/o Jno. J. Hurley & Paulina Cole
    par. b. Hawkins Co., TN & Ows.; R.Lee

JAMESON
Sarilda, 16 Oct., 1878 (F W alive Lee)
    d/o J[ohn] D. Jameson & Sarah J. Spencer
    par. b. Lee & Lee; R.Lee
    [a/L as Errilda Neva, b. 15 Nov, 1878,
    d/o John D.; par. both b. Ows.; rest of
    data same.]
JEWELL
Wesley, 9 July, 1878 (M W alive Lee)
    s/o David Jewell & Lucinda R. Johnson
    par. b. Clay & Lee Co., VA; R.Lee
    [David & Lucinda md. 11 Dec., 1871 Lee]
JOHNSON
Naoma E., 30 July, 1875 (F W alive Lee)
    d/o Wilburn Johnson & Zerilda Bowman
    par. b. Ashe Co., NC & Ows.; R.Lee
Robert, 15 July, 1875 (M W alive Lee)
    s/o Timothy Johnson & Sally Ann Pitman
    par. b. Est. & Est.; R.Lee
Zachary M., 27 Dec., 1875 (M W alive Lee)
    s/o Samuel Johnson & Zarilda McGuire
    par. b. Let. & Ows.; R.Lee
JONES
Breckenridge, 2 March, 1874 (M W alive Br.)
    s/o John Jones & Nancy Buckheart
    par. b. Morg. & Lee Co., VA; R.Lee
Gilly Ann, 22 Sept., 1876 (F W alive Lee)
    d/o John Jones & Nancy Buckhart
    par. b. Morg. & Lee Co., VA; R.Lee
John T., 29 March, 1876 (M W alive Lee)
    s/o Stephen M. Jones & Mary Tipton
    par. b. Lee Co., VA & Est.; R.Lee [see
    deaths]
Llew Ellen, 30 Aug., 1878 (F W alive Lee)
    d/o John Jones & Nancy Buckhart
    par. b. Morg. & Harl.; R.Lee

JUDD
Lilly Ann, 24 March, 1874 (F W alive Lee)
    d/o [James] Rowland Judd & Nancy Palmer
    par. b. Ows. & Br.; R.Lee
    [listed in deaths as "Biddy A."]
Manda, 16 Nov., 1878 (F W alive Lee)
    d/o James R. Judd & Nancy "Farmer"
    par. b. Ows. & Ows.; R.Lee
Martha B., 16 Nov., 1876 (F W alive Lee)
    d/o J[ames] R. Judd & Nancy Palmer
    par. b. Ows. & Br.; R.Lee   [see deaths]

KELLY
Thomas J., 20 June, 1878 (M W alive Lee)
    s/o Speed S. Kelly & Margaret A. Smyth
    par. b. Est. & Ows.; R.Lee
Wm. J., 31 Oct., 1875 (M W alive Lee)
    s/o John S. Kelly & Charlottie Wright
    par. b. Ows. & Ows.; R.Lee
KIDD
Elijah F., 16 Sept., 1874 (M W alive Lee)
    s/o Samuel Kidd & Elvira King
    par. b. Br. & Br.; R.Lee
    [John Saml. & Elmira md. c1868 Br.]
Mariam S., 3 Sept., 1876 (F W alive Lee)
    d/o David Kidd & Lourana King
    par. b. Br. & Br.; R.Lee
KILBURN
Catharine, 25 April, 1878 (F W alive Lee)
    d/o Tipton Kilburn & Christina Combs
    par. b. Hanc. Co., TN & Br.; R.Lee
    [listed twice]
Greenberry, 27 June, 1875 (M W alive Lee)
    s/o Tipton Kilburn & Christenia Combs
    par. b. Hanc. Co., TN & Br.; R.Lee
KINCAID
Alice M., 22 Feb., 1878 (F W alive Lee)
    d/o Plummer Kincaid & Gilly Ann Cockerham
    par. b. Lee & Wlf.; R.Lee
Douglas, 24 July, 1878 (M W alive Lee)
    s/o Socrates Kincaid & Cynthiann Trimble
    par. b. Est. & Montg.; R.Lee
Dudley H., 17 May, 1875 (M W alive Lee)
    s/o Edward Kincaid & Emily J. Cable
    par. b. Ows. & Ows.; R.Lee

KINCAID (cont.)
John E., 17 Oct., 1875 (M W alive Lee)
    s/o Edward D. Kincaid & Luvina Gray
    par. b. Est. & Ows.; R.Lee
    [a/L same date 1876]
Malissa, 25 Nov., 1876 (F W alive Lee)
    d/o Edward Kincaid & Emily Cable
    par. b. Ows. & Ows.; R.Lee
Robert B., 1 April, 1878 (M W alive Lee)
    s/o Edward Kincaid & Emily J. Cable
    par. b. Ows. & Ows.; R.Lee
KING
nn, 18 May, 1874 (M W dead Lee)
    s/o Green C. King & Sarah J. Tolby
    par. b. Br. & Br.; R.Lee
    [Green & Sarah md. 6 May, 1873, Lee]
Alwilda, 1 Dec., 1876 (F W alive Lee)
    d/o Atison C. King & Anna Tolby
    par b. Wlf. & Wlf.; R.Lee   [see deaths]
Emiline, 25 March, 1876 (F W alive Lee)
    d/o Green K[elly] King & Melissa J. White
    par. b. Wlf. & Wlf.; R.Lee
William, 28 April, 1874 (M W alive Lee)
    s/o Atison King & Ann Tolby
    par. b. Br. & Br.; R.Lee
KIRK
-----, 20 June, 1878 (F W dead Lee)
    d/o Wm. G. Kirk & Mahaley Williams [see
    mgs.]; par. b. Fleming & Per.; R.Lee

LANE
James D., 29 April, 1876 (M W alive Lee)
    s/o John M. Lane & Orfa E. Smith
    par. b. Scott Co, VA & Est; R.Lee
LOCKARD
Wm. P., 10 Nov., 1874 (M W alive Lee)
    s/o Wm. Lockard & Eliz. Garland
    par. b. Knox & Claiborne Co, TN; R.Lee
LONGSWORTH
Wm. E., 29 Aug., 1875 (M W alive Lee)
    s/o Geo. Longsworth & Jane Pitman
    par. b. Claiborne Co., TN & Ows.; R.Lee
    [Geo. & Jane md. 22 Oct., 1874 Lee]
LUCAS
nn, 23 Dec., 1875 (F W dead Lee)
    d/o Samuel R. Lucas & Winnie Thompson
    par. b. Lee Co, VA & Lee Co, VA; R.Lee

22

LUCAS (cont.)
Francis M., 7 April, 1878 (M W alive Lee)
    s/o Jesse Lucas & Mary Ann Jameson
    par. b. Lee Co, VA & Est.; R.Lee
James C., 20 Aug., 1874 (M W alive Lee)
    s/o Pleasant Lucas & Elenor C. Markham
    par. b. Lee Co, VA & Lee Co, VA; R.Lee
Lydia E., 16 July, 1875 (F W alive Lee)
    d/o Wm. B. Lucas & Harriet Arnold
    par. b. Lee Co., VA & Hanc. Co., TN; R.Lee
    [Wm. & Harriet md. 23 Jan., 1873 Lee]
Wm. D., 11 June, 1878 (M W alive Lee)
    s/o [James] Robt. Lucas & Cyntha Olinger
    par. b. Lee Co, VA & Lee Co, VA; R.Lee
LUTES
Andrew J., 12 Oct., 1878 (M W alive Lee)
    s/o John Lutes & Lucinda Gum
    par. b. Ows. & Ows.; R.Lee
    [appar. d. before the 1880 census]
    [John & Lucinda md. 31 Dec., 1871 Lee]
Horace G., 17 Aug., 1875 (M W alive Lee)
    s/o John Lutes & Lucinda Gum
    par. b. Ows. & Ows.; R.Lee
LYNCH
Harvey, 20 July, 1878 (M W alive Lee)
    s/o Thomas H. Lynch & Nancy Brandenburgh
    par. b. Orange Co., KY [NC] & Est.; R.Lee
    [NOTE: There is no Orange Co., KY; he was
    b. NC, per 1880 census]
LYONS
George A., 26 Aug., 1874 (M W alive Jess.)
    s/o Wm. Lyons & Hariet Stafford
    par. b. DeKalb Co., AL & Clark; R.Lee

McCLURE/McLURE
James M., 15 July, 1878 (M W alive Lee)
    s/o James M. McLure & Lucy Barnett
    par. b. Scott Co, VA & Scott Co, VA; R.Lee
Samuel, 11 Jan., 1874 (M W alive Lee)
    s/o James McClure & Lucy Barnett
    Scott Co., VA & Scott Co., VA; R.Lee
McGUIRE
Catherine, 25 May, 1875 (F W alive Lee)
    d/o Warwick McGuire & Cath. Akers
    par. b. Est. & Est.; R.Lee
    [Warwick md. Cath. 29 Dec, 1864 Ows. - RJB]

23

McGUIRE (cont.)
Charles, 25 April, 1876 (M W alive Lee)
    s/o A. B. McGuire & Helen Treadway
    par. b. Est. & Clay; R.Lee
    [Arch & Helen md. 21 Dec., 1865 Ows. - RJB]
Julia A., 19 Oct., 1875 (F W alive Lee)
    d/o Archibald McGuire & Cath. Davis
    par. b. Est. & Mason; R.Lee
    [Arch md. Cath. 24 Dec, 1874 Lee]
Lucy B., 8 June, 1875 (F W alive Lee)
    d/o Felix G. McGuire & Mattie Dixon
    par. b. Ows. & Mason; R.Lee
    [Felix & Mattie md. Aug., 1873 Lee]
Martha F., 12 Dec., 1878 (F W alive Lee)
    d/o Joseph McGuire & Evaline Akers
    par. b. Ows. & Ows.; R.Lee
    [Jos. md. Evaline 12 Sept., 1869 - RJB]
Milton, 26 Jan., 1874 (M W alive Lee)
    s/o Thomas McGuire & Margarett Thomas
    par. b. Est. & Ows.; R.Lee
    [Thos. md. Margt. 16 Sept, 1869 Ows. - RJB]
Monroe, 10 April, 1874 (M W alive Lee)
    s/o Archd. B. McGuire & Helen Treadway
    par. b. Est. & Clay; R.Lee; [remarks
    unreadable]
McKINNIE
Samuel J., 14 Oct., 1876 (M W alive Lee)
    s/o James B. McKinnie & Sarah A. Calimes
    par. b. Est. & Br.; R.Lee
McQUEEN
James M., 6 June, 1875 (M W alive Lee)
    s/o Samuel McQueen & Phebe A. Parsons
    par. b. Johnson Co, TN & Lee Co, VA; R.Lee
Wm., 30 Sept., 1875 (M - alive Lee)
    s/o John McQueen & Nancy Crawford
    par. b. ------

MALONEY
Cora, 20 March, 1874 (F W alive Lee)
    d/o George Maloney & Mildred A. Blount
    par. b. Ows. & Ows.; R.Lee
Flora, 4 Oct., 1878 (F W alive Lee)
    d/o Franklin "L" Maloney & Emeline Willis
    par. b. Ows. & Clay; R.Lee
    [see mgs. for Franklin P. & Mary E.]

MALONEY (cont.)
Lucy A., 22 Feb., 1875 (F W alive Lee)
    d/o John Maloney & Margret Hays
    par. b. Est. & Est.; R.Lee
Sarah, 12 Jan., 1876 (F W alive Lee)
    d/o George Maloney & "Millard" A. Blount
    par. b. Ows. & Ows.; R.Lee
Thomps[on], 13 April, 1878 (M W alive Lee)
    s/o Wm. Maloney & Lew Ellen Gum
    par. b. Wlf. & Ows.; R.Lee
    [Wm. & Lou Ellen md. 5 March, 1874 Lee]
William C., 30 June, 1878 (M W alive Lee)
    s/o George Maloney & Mildred Blount
    par. b. Ows. & Ows.; R.Lee
MANARD
Mary, 4 June, 1874 (F W alive Martin Co, KY)
    d/o Joseph E. Manard & Nancy Slone
    par. b. Johnson & Pike; R.Lee
MANN
Demia, 12 Dec., 1874 (F W alive Lee)
    d/o Wm. S. Mann & Helen J. Roberts
    par. b. Est. & Ows.; R.Lee
    [apparently d. pre-1880]
James M., 7 Oct., 1875 (M W alive Lee)
    s/o Wm. MALONEY & Arminda Mann
    par. b. Lee & Lee; R.Lee [apparently
    illegitimate]
MARKHAM
nn [Edwin], 10 Nov., 1875 (M W alive Lee)
    s/o James D. Markham & Lurana Hays
    par. b. Lee Co., VA & Clay; R.Lee
    [James & Lurana md. 15 Dec., 1857 Br.]
MARSHALL
Virginia B., 4 Sept., 1878 (F W alive Lee)
    d/o Heny(?) Marshall & Margaret Couch
    par. b. Lee Co., VA & Br.; R.Lee
    ["H.C." & Margaret md 18 Dec, 1878 Lee]
MARTIN
Sidney, 19 Feb., 1879 [1878] (M W alive Lee)
    s/o Elisha Martin & Nancy E. Robinson
    par. b. Scott Co., VA & Ows; R.Lee
    [Elisha & Nancy md. 12 Dec., 1872 Lee]
    [NOTE: This birth listed as 1879, but the
    others on this page were 1878; also Sidney
    is age 2 in 1880 census]

MAYS/MAISE/MAIZE/MAZE
Henry, 20 Aug., 1874 (M W alive Lee)
    s/o Andrew Mays & Racheal Mays
    par b. Per. & Per.; R.Lee
    [listed in deaths as "Harvey" Mays]
Nancy, 9 March, 1875 (F W alive Lee)
    d/o Abijah Maize & Joanna Watts
    par. b. Br. & Br.; R.Lee
    ["Hijah" & Joannah md. c1865 Br.]
Nathaniel, 10 Sept., 1875 (M W alive Lee)
    s/o Henry Maise & Rachel Maise
    par. b. Br. & Br.; R.Lee
William, ----- [1878] (M W alive Lee)
    s/o Henry Maze & Rachel Maze
    par. b. Br. & Br.; R.Lee
MILLER
-----, 15 Sept., 1878 (M W alive Lee)
    s/o Josiah Miller & Arrela Johnson
    par. b. Br. & Wlf.; R.Lee   [see deaths]
Ida, 5 Nov., 1878 (F W alive Lee)
    d/o Wm. L. Miller & Polina Rose
    par. b. Br. & Br.; R.Lee
    [Wm. Letcher & Polina md. 1873 Br.]
Mathias N., 12 Sept., 1876 (M W alive Lee)
    s/o Wm. L. Miller & Paulina Rose
    par. b. Br. & Est.; R.Lee
Owen, 22 March, 1874 (M W alive Lee)
    s/o George Miller & Louisa Shackelford
    par. b. Br. & Br.; R.Lee
    [Geo. & Louisa md. c1866 Br.]
Stephen, 20 Dec., 1878 (M W alive Lee)
    s/o Elhannon Miller & Florence E. Johnson
    [see mgs.]; par. b. Br. & Pow.; R.Lee
MORRIS
Archibald, - Oct., 1876 (M W alive Lee)
    s/o Joseph Morris & Lucinda Spencer
    par. b. Per. & Ows.; R.Lee

NEWMAN
nn, 16 July, 1875 (M W dead Lee)
    s/o Morris Newman & Lucinda Newman
    par. b. Clark & Stokes Co, NC; R.Lee; twin
nn, 16 July, 1875 (M W dead Lee)
    s/o Morris Newman & Lucinda Newman
    par. b. Clark & Stokes Co, NC; R.Lee; twin

NEWMAN (cont.)
Katty, 5 Aug., 1874 (F W alive Lee)
    d/o Elias Newman & Mary Smallwood
    par. b. Clark & Ows.; R.Lee
Nancy M., 25 Aug., 1875 (F W alive Ows.)
    d/o John W. Newman & Ellen F. Partington
    par. b. Ows. & Ows.; R.Lee
NEWTON
Godfrey, 5 Aug., 1876 (M W alive Lee)
    s/o John Newton & Julia A. Durbin
    par. b. Ows. & Ows.; R.Lee
Henry, 20 Feb., 1878 (M W alive Lee)
    s/o Richard Newton & Nancy Ashcraft
    par. b. Ows. & Est.; R.Lee
Jordan, 19 Sept., 1876 (M W alive Lee)
    s/o Wm. Newton & Mary E. Wyatt
    par. b. Ows. & Est.; R.Lee
Rachel, 24 Dec., 1876 (F W alive Lee)
    d/o Decatur Newton & Martha J. Freeman
    par. b. Ows. & Est.; R.Lee
NOLEN
Georgella, 4 Jan., 1874 (F W alive Lee)
    d/o Henry Nolen & Christina Miller
    par. b. Mad. & Br.; R.Lee
    [Henry & Christina md. c1871 Br.]

OLDHAM
John M., 30 Jan., 1876 (M W alive Lee)
    s/o Lewis C. Oldham & Rhoda Hamilton
    par. b. Boone & Ows.; R.Lee
OLINGER
Ira, 28 Oct., 1875 (M W alive Lee)
    s/o Daniel Olinger & Phoebe Trouse
    par. b. Lee Co., VA & Lee Co., VA; R.Lee
OLIVER
Gilford H., 10 July, 1878 (M W alive Lee)
    s/o Samuel P. Oliver & Eliz. Shackelford
    par. b. Ows. & Br.; R.Lee
John R., 25 Feb., 1878 (M W alive Lee)
    s/o George Oliver & Malvan Chambers
    par. b. Ows. & Ows; R.Lee [see deaths]
Luther W. T., 16 Aug., 1874 (M W alive Lee)
    s/o Samuel Oliver & Eliz. Shackleford
    par. b. Ows. & Br.; R.Lee
Saml. E., 6 July, 1876 (M W alive Lee)
    s/o Saml. P. Oliver & Eliz. Shackelford
    par. b. Ows. & Br.; R.Lee

OLIVER (cont.)
---- [Wm.], 23 Sept., 1876 (M W alive Lee)
    s/o Geo. C. Oliver & Malvina J. Chambers
    par. b. Ows. & Br.; R.Lee
    [Geo. & Malvina md. 26 June, 1873 Lee;
    Malvina appar. d. pre-1880]

PALMER/PARMER
Archibald, 8 Dec., 1875 (M W alive Lee)
    s/o John Palmer & Vina Coomer
    par. b. Br. & Lee Co., VA; R.Lee
Cordelia, 26 Oct., 1878 (F W alive Lee)
    d/o Reubin Parmer & Maranda Bowman
    par. b. Lee Co., VA & Br.; R.Lee
    [Reubin & Maranda md. 19 Oct., 1857 Br.]
Elender, 4 March, 1874 (F W alive Lee)
    d/o James Palmer & "Varina" Combs
    par. b. Hanc. Co., TN & Br.; R.Lee
George C., 29 May, 1876 (M W alive Lee)
    s/o Reubin Palmer & Miranda Bowman
    par. b. Stokes Co., NC & Br.; R.Lee
    [appar. d. before the 1880 census]
Mary E., 26 Feb., 1876 (F W alive Lee)
    d/o James M. Palmer & "Farinda" Combs
    par. b. Ows. & Br.; R.Lee
Mary, 27 Oct., 1878 (F W alive Lee)
    d/o Green Parmer & Manda Webb
    par. b. Ows. & Ows; R.Lee
    [Green & Manda md. 23 Feb., 1876 Lee]
PHILLIPS
nn, 15 Dec., 1875 (M W dead Lee)
    s/o Wm. J. Phillips & Eliz. Winkle
    par. b. Ows. & Est.; R.Lee
    [Wm. & Eliz. md. 5 Aug., 1873 Lee]
Adam A. [Adda M.], 15 Jan., 1878 (F W al. Lee)
    d/o Thomas J. Phillips & Frances J. McGuire
    par. b. Ows. & Ows.; R.Lee
Henry F., 3 Aug., 1874 (M W alive Lee)
    s/o Thos. J. Phillips & Frances J. McGuire
    par. b. Ows. & Ows.; R.Lee
PIGG
Eveline, 29 Dec., 1874 (F W alive Lee)
    d/o Jackson Pigg & Nancy Smith
    par. b. Clay & Ows.; R.Lee
Thomas J., - Sept., 1876 (M W alive Lee)
    s/o Remus Pigg & Nancy Smith
    par. b. Clay & Jackson Co.; R.Lee

PITMAN
nn, 29 July, 1875 (F? W dead Lee)
    ch/o Jesse Pitman & Polly Estes
    par. b. Ows. & Est.; R.Lee
Rosa F., 28 July, 1878 (F W alive Lee)
    d/o John COLE & Gilly Ann Pitman
    par. b. Ows. & Ows.; R.Lee [apparently
    illegitimate]
PLOWMAN
Albert, 9 Feb., 1876 (M W alive Lee)
    s/o Theophilus Plowman & Sallie Sparks
    par. b. Est. & Est.; R.Lee
PRICHARD/PRITCHARD
Annie E., 7 July, 1875 (F W alive Lee)
    d/o John M. CORNETT & Rutha J. Prichard
    par. b. Scott Co., VA & Ows; R.Lee;
    illegitimate
Joseph, 11 July, 1874 (M W alive Lee)
    s/o Jilson Pritchard & Eliz. Holland
    par. b. Ows. & uk; R.Lee
PROFITT
Elijah, 9 July, 1875 (M W alive Lee)
    s/o Eli Profitt & Mary A. Spencer
    par. b. Let. & Per.; R.Lee
James M., 7 March, 1876 (M W alive Lee)
    s/o James D. Profitt & Eliz. Jameson
    par. b. Ows. & Est.; R.Lee
Jesse F., 12 July,1875 (M W alive Lee)
    s/o Wm. M. Profitt & Mary J. Kincannon
    par. b. Let. & Smith Co., VA; R.Lee
    [Wm. & Mary md. 2 Oct., 1870 Lee]
Patience, 12 March, 1875 (F W alive Lee)
    d/o James D. Profitt & Eliz. Jameson
    par. b. Ows. & Est.; R.Lee
nn [Wilgus], 24 April, 1875 (M W alive Lee)
    s/o Ira G. Profitt & Patience Jameson
    par. b. Per. & Rockc.; R.Lee
PRYSE
Viola, 27 Sept., 1875 (F W alive Lee)
    d/o David Pryse & Lucy A. Brandenburgh
    par. b. Pnnylly(?), Wales & Est.; R.Lee
Zacheriah T., 18 Sept., 1876 (M W alive Est.)
    s/o Elias M. Pryse & Eliz. Bowman
    par. b. Wales & GA; R.Lee

QUILLEN
Harlan, 1 Aug., 1876 (M W alive Lee)
    s/o Chas. A. Quillen & Delina Brandenburgh
    par. b. Scott Co., VA & Ows.; R.Lee

REED
John F., 29 June, 1875 (M W alive Lee)
    s/o Geo. M. Reed & Matilda Murill
    par. b. Est. & Est.; R.Lee
Mary, 28 July, 1876 (F W alive Lee)
    d/o Enoch Reed & Rebecca Bush
    par. b. Est. & Wlf.; R.Lee
Shelton B., 2 March, 1875 (M W alive Lee)
    s/o Weber H. Reed & Jane E. Beatty
    par. b. Mad. & Franklin Co., MO; R.Lee
REESE
Francis, 2 July, 1876 (M W alive Lee)
    s/o Elijah Reese & Sarah A. Richardson
    par. b. TN & Est.; R.Lee
Zerilda, 6 March, 1874 (F W alive Lee)
    d/o Elijah C. Reese & Sally A. Richardson
    par. b. Hawkins Co., TN & Est.; R.Lee
RILEY
Zachary, 3 April, 1876 (M W alive Lee)
    s/o James Riley & Nancy Estep
    par. b. Br. & Harl.; R.Lee
ROACH
George W., 12 Sept., 1878 (M W alive Lee)
    s/o Wm. H. Roach & Rebecca Isaacs
    par. b. Ows. & Jack.; R.Lee
John, 15 Nov., 1878 (M W alive Lee)
    s/o Ance Roach & Margaret Combs
    par. b. Mad. & Per.; R.Lee
    [Anderson & Margaret md. 20 Nov., 1875 Lee]
Sylvester, 15 March,1878 ("F" W alive Pend)
    ch/o Thos. J. Roach & Cath. E. Wood
    par. b. Ows. & Pend.; R.Lee
Thomas, 18 March, 1876 (M W alive Lee)
    s/o Anderson Roach & Margret Combs
    par. b. Mad. & Per.; R.Lee
ROBERTS
Lucinda, 20 April, 1874 (F W alive Lee)
    d/o Moses Roberts & Nancy E. Burns
    par. b. Clay & Clay; R.Lee
    [Moses & Nancy md. 22 Feb., 1858, Br.]

ROBERTS (cont.)
Nancy, 31 Dec., 1876 (F W alive Lee)
    d/o Moses Roberts & Nancy Burns
    par. b. Est. & IN; R.Lee
    [appar. d. before the 1880 census]
ROGERS
Mattie J., 23 Jan., 1876 (F W alive Lee)
    d/o Isaac T. Rogers & Amanda Reed
    par. b. Pow. & IN; R.Lee
ROSS
nn, 11 June, 1874 (F W alive Lee)
    d/o Philip HAMMAN & Emily Ross
    par. b. Morg. & Ows; R.Lee; illegitimate
Millard, 20 July, 1874 (M W alive Lee)
    s/o Henry Ross & Delina Brandenburgh
    par. b. Ows. & Ows.; R.Lee

SCHOLL
Larry(?) Lee, 8 Dec., 1878 (M W alive Lee)
    s/o Wm. C. Scholl & Ella McGuire
    par. b. Clark & Ows.; R.Lee
SHACKELFORD
James A., 25 July, 1878 (M W alive Lee)
    s/o M. E. Shackelford & Mary Ann Kincaid
    par. b. Br. & Ows.; R.Lee
Santford, 1 April, 1876 (M W alive Lee)
    s/o Mandrel E. Shackelford & Mariam S.
    Kincaid; par. b. Br. & Ows.; R.Lee
SHEPARD
Franklin W., 5 Dec., 1878 (M W alive Lee)
    s/o Emmon L. Shepard & Rebecca C. Jones
    [see mgs]; par.b. Golia Co, VA; Lee Co, VA;
    R.Lee [NOTE: There is no Golia Co., VA]
SHOEMAKER
Daniel K., 22 Feb., 1874 (M W alive Lee)
    s/o Andrew B. Shoemaker & [Margt.] Eveline
    Baker; par. b. Lee Co., VA & Ows.; R.Lee
Milliades [Millard], 24 April, 1875 (M W al.
    Lee) s/o Thomas Shoemaker & Sabra Lewis
    par. b. Lee Co., VA & Per.; R.Lee
Uller, 15 June, 1878 (F W alive Lee)
    d/o Andrew B. Shoemaker & [Margt.] Evoline
    Baker; par. b. Lee Co., VA & Ows.; R.Lee
William, 10 May, 1875 (M W alive Lee)
    s/o Henry Shoemaker & Henna(?) Williams
    [see mgs.]; par. b. Ows. & Per.; R.Lee

31

SHOEMAKER (cont.)
Woodford M., 3 April, 1876 (M W alive Lee)
    s/o Andrew B. Shoemaker & Evaline Baker
    par. b. Lee Co., VA & Est.; R.Lee
SLONE
Mary L., 3 Jan., 1874 (F W alive Lee)
    d/o Wm. D. Slone & Zerilda Howard
    par. b. Pike & Est.; R.Lee
William, 26 April, 1878 (M W alive Lee)
    s/o Wm. D. Slone & Sarilda Howard
    par. b. Pike & Est.; R.Lee [d. Dec., 1879]
SMALLWOOD
Elizabeth, 11 April, 1876 (F W alive Lee)
    d/o David E. Smallwood & Lucy A. Gorden
    par. b. Ows. & Ows.; R.Lee
Louania, 6 Jan., 1874 (F W alive Lee)
    d/o John Smallwood & Rosilla Jones
    par. b. Ows. & VA; R.Lee
SMITH/SMYTH
----, 7 Feb., "1879" [1878] (M W dead Lee)
    s/o Henry Smith & Polly Roberts
    par. b. Ows. & Ows.; R.Lee [appar. twin
    of Clay; listed in deaths 7 Feb, 1878]
Charley B., 9 Sept., 1878 (M W alive Lee)
    s/o John M. Smyth & Lucy E. Williams [see
    mgs.]; par. b. Est. & Est.; R.Lee
Clay, 7 Feb., 1878 (M W alive Lee)
    s/o Henry Smith & Polly Roberts
    par. b. Ows. & Ows.; R.Lee [appar. twin]
Felix, 17 June, 1874 (M W alive Lee)
    s/o Asa Smith & Sophia Brandenburgh
    par. b. Ows. & Ows.; R.Lee
George C., 25 Nov., 1876 (M W alive Lee)
    s/o John M. Smith & Lucy E. Williams
    par. b. Est. & Est.; R.Lee
George W., 18 May, 1875 (M W alive Lee)
    s/o Abraham Smyth & --- [Caroline] "Fowler"
    par. b. Lee Co., VA & "Taswell", NC; R.Lee
Hiram U.S. Grant, 20 Nov, 1878 (M W alive Lee)
    s/o Isaac Smyth & Tabitha Ross
    par. b. Let. & Ows.; R.Lee
James E., 12 Dec., 1878 (M W alive Lee)
    s/o Abraham Smyth & Caroline "Farmer"
    par. b. Lee & Caswell Co., NC; R.Lee
Julia, 28 Sept., 1875 (F W alive Lee)
    d/o Huram Smith & Eda Roberts
    par. b. Ows. & Ows.; R.Lee

SMITH/SMYTH (cont.)
Keen F., 28 Aug., 1874 (M W alive Lee)
    s/o John M. Smith & --------
    par. b. Est. & Let.; R.Lee
SNOWDEN
Alex., 26 Feb., 1878 (M W alive Lee)
    s/o John M. Snowden & Lydia Thompson [see
    mgs.]; par. b. Ows. & Ows.; R.Lee
Dora, 28 April, 1876 (F W alive Lee)
    d/o John M. Snowden & Lidia Thompson
    par. b. Ows. & Ows.; R.Lee
Enos, 31 July, 1876 (M W alive Lee)
    s/o F[rancis] M. Snowden & Polly Thompson
    par. b. Est. & Lee Co., VA; R.Lee
SPARKS
Henry, 9 May, 1876 (M W alive Lee)
    s/o Sylvester Sparks & Nancy Ashcraft
    par. b. Est. & Est.; R.Lee
Joseph, 29 March, 1878 (M W alive Lee)
    s/o Thomas S. Sparks & Eliz. Durbin
    par. b. Est. & Est.; R.Lee
SPENCER
Deborah, 22 May, 1874 (F W alive Lee)
    d/o Nicholas B. Spencer & Mary J. Stamper
    par. b. Ows. & Ows.; R.Lee
    [Nicholas Bowman & Mary Jane md. c1859 Br.]
Eulia, 5 Nov., 1876 (F W alive Lee)
    d/o Geo. W. Spencer & Margaret Hobbs
    par. b. Ows. & Lee Co., VA; R.Lee
Isaiah, 30 April, 1878 (M W alive Lee)
    s/o Geo. W. Spencer & Margaret E. Hobbs
    par. b. Wlf. & Lee Co., VA; R.Lee
    [apparently d. pre-1880]
Isham, 2 July, 1878 (M W alive Lee)
    s/o Moses Spencer & "Ella" M. Gum
    par. b. Ows. & Ows.; R.Lee
    [Moses & Edy md. 25 Nov., 1870 Lee]
Jesse C., 23 May, 1875 (M W alive Lee)
    s/o Wm. S. Spencer & Mary A. Gum
    par. b. Ows. & Ows.; R.Lee
Margaret E., 24 Nov, 1878 (F W alive Lee)
    d/o Nicholas Spencer & Mary J. Stamper
    par. b. Wlf. & Wlf.; R.Lee
Sanford, 4 Sept., 1876 (M W alive Lee)
    s/o Nicholas Spencer & Mary J. Stamper
    par. b. Est. & Ows.; R.Lee

SPENCER (cont.)

Wm. F., 15 July, 1878 (M W alive Lee)
    s/o Simeon Spencer & Margaret Bumgardner
    par. b. Ows. & Wythe Co., VA; R.Lee
    (a/L 21 June, 1878)

SPICER

Polly, 23 Nov., 1875 (F W alive Lee)
    d/o Samuel Spicer & Eliza [Ellis] Stamper
    par. b. Br. & Br.; R.Lee

STACY

Genilla [Geniva], 30 Dec, 1874 (F W alive Lee)
    d/o Martin Stacy & Alba France
    par. b. Br. & Lee Co., VA; R.Lee

Rosa C., 21 May, 1874 (F W alive Lee)
    d/o Wm. Stacy & Melvina Slone
    par. b. uk & uk; R.Lee

Zarilda J., 1 March, 1876 (F W alive Lee)
    d/o Wm. Stacy & Melvina Slone
    par. b. uk & uk; R.Lee

STAMPER

Dora B., 5 Dec., 1878 (F W alive Lee)
    d/o Millard F. Stamper & Edda Townsend
    par. b. Ows. & Pow.; R.Lee

Earley, 30 Oct., 1875 (M W alive Lee)
    s/o Edward Stamper & Tildy Turner
    par. b. Clay & Br.; R.Lee
    [Edw. & Matilda md. 10 April, 1859 Br.]

Florence [Floyd], 9 Dec., 1878 (M W alive Lee)
    s/o Wm. L. Stamper & Sylvana Crawford
    par. b. Br. & Ows.; R.Lee
    [Wm. & Sylvana md. 13 June, 1872 Lee]

Geo. W., 1 Sept., 1874 (M W alive Lee)
    s/o Joel Stamper & Sally A. Cockrum(?)
    par. b. Ows. & Ows.; R.Lee

John A., 3 Nov., 1875 (M W alive Lee)
    s/o James A. Stamper & Judith Tolby
    par. b. Morg. & Est.; R.Lee

Loueller, 16 April, 1878 (F W alive Br.)
    d/o John E. Stamper & Eliz. Lossen
    par. b. Lee & Lee; R.Br.
    [John & Eliz. Grace md. 1870 Br.]

Mary A., 11 Jan., 1874 (F W alive Wlf)
    d/o Joseph Stamper & Cynthia Cabell
    par. b. Ows. & Ows.; R.Lee
    [Jos. & Cynthia Caroline md. 6 April, 1871
    Lee]

STAMPER (cont.)
Mary J., 5 Feb., 1875 (F W alive Wlf)
    d/o Millard "M." Stamper & Ada Townsend
    par. b. Ows. & Wlf.; R.Lee
Saml. M., 26 June, 1876 (M W alive Lee)
    s/o Joel Stamper & Sallie A. Conun(?)
    par. b. Ows. & Ows.; R.Lee
---- [Susan], 17 April, 1878 (F W alive Lee)
    d/o Edward Stamper & Matilda Turner
    par. b. Clay & Br.; R.Lee
STEEL
Margret, 27 June, 1875 (F W alive Lee)
    d/o Daniel Steel & Polly Cole
    par. b. Stokes Co., NC & Ows.; R.Lee
Thomas A., 18 Feb., 1878 (M W alive Lee)
    s/o Wm. Steel & Patsy Jameson
    par. b. Stokes Co., NC & Est.; R.Lee
STERNBERG
Felix, 21 March, 1876 (M W alive Lee)
    s/o Saml. Sternberg & Mahaley Robinson
    par. b. PA & Ows.; R.Lee
STRONG
Andrew B., 9 April, 1878 (M W alive Lee)
    s/o Alex. Strong & Sarah J. Chambers
    par. b. Br. & Morg.; R.Lee
    [Alex & Sarah md. c1861 Br.]
Lydia, 8 Nov., 1875 (F W alive Lee)
    d/o Alex. Strong & Sarah Chambers
    par. b. Morg. & Br.; R.Lee
Nancy D., 13 June, 1876 (F W alive Lee)
    d/o Thomas Strong & Evaline Spicer
    par. b. Br. & Br.; R.Lee

TEWART
James, 5 June, 1874 (M W alive Lee)
    s/o Robt. Tewart & Polly A. McGuire
    par. b. Durham Co., England & Ows; R.Lee;
    twin
Lucy, 5 June, 1874 (F W alive Lee)
    d/o Robt. Tewart & Polly A. McGuire
    par. b. Durham Co., England & Ows; R.Lee;
    twin

THACKER
Sallie, 26 Oct., 1876 (F W alive Lee)
    d/o James W. Thacker & Martha Steel
    par. b. Lee Co., VA & Ows.; R.Lee
    [James & Martha md. 15 Aug., 1873 Lee]
THARPE
Jesse, 28 Feb., 1876 (M W alive Lee)
    s/o Oliver Tharpe & Rebecca Ragan
    par. b. Lee Co, VA & Kent(?) Co., TN; R.Lee
    [NOTE: There is no Kent Co., TN]
    [Oliver & Rebecca md. c1858 Br.]
THOMAS
Emma M., - April, 1874 (F W alive Lee)
    d/o Wm. Thomas & Susan McGuire
    par. b. Nicholas & Johnson Co., MO; R.Lee
Joseph P., 9 Dec., 1875 (M W alive Lee)
    s/o James M. Thomas & Cath. Thompson [see
    mgs.]; par. b. Ows. & Ows.; R.Lee
    [Eleanor Cath. d. 12 days after Joseph's
    birth - see deaths]
Martha, 19 Feb., 1878 (F W alive Lee)
    d/o Henry H. Thomas & Jane P. Shoemaker
    par. b. Est. & Lee Co., VA; R.Lee
Stella, 7 Oct., 1876 (F W alive Lee)
    d/o Henry Thomas & Jane Shoemaker
    par. b. Est. & Lee; R.Lee
THOMPSON
Nancy M., 27 Aug., 1878 (F W alive Lee)
    d/o Wm. P. Thompson & Sarah E. Lucas
    par. b. Lee Co., VA & Lee Co., VA; R.Lee
TINCHER
Albert, 25 March, 1876 (M W alive Lee)
    s/o Asa Tincher & Sarah Estes
    par. b. Clark & Ows.; R.Lee
Felix, 21 Jan., 1878 (M W alive Lee)
    s/o Asa Tincher & Sarah Estes
    par. b. Clark & Ows.; R.Lee
Henry E[tta], 21 March, 1878 ("M" W alive Lee)
    d/o Randall Tincher & Rebecca A. Howell
    par. b. Ows. & Ows.; R.Lee
    [Randy & Rebecca md. 11 Jan., 1872 Lee]
Nancy, 27 Oct., 1876 (F W alive Lee)
    d/o James Tincher & Susanah Gordon
    par. b. Est. & VA; R.Lee
Wm. H., 18 Feb., 1875 (M W alive Lee)
    s/o Randolf Tincher & Rebecca A. Howell
    par. b. Ows. & Ows.; R.Lee

TOWNSEND
nn, 6 Nov., 1875 (F - ----- ---)
    d/o unknown & "Rus" Townsend; par. b. ----
Jerry T., 26 Dec., 1876 (M W alive Lee)
    s/o Geo. Townsend & Sena Profitt [see mgs.]
    par. b. Morg. & Ows.; R.Lee
Sarah(?), 6 Aug., 1875 (F W alive Lee)
    d/o James Townsend & Margaret Strange
    par. b. Wlf. & Est.; R.Lee
TREADWAY
----- [Geo. C.], 28 Nov., 1878 (M W alive Lee)
    s/o Wm. M Treadway & Mary F[rances] Briscoe
    [see mg]; par. b. Ows & Hanc. Co, TN; R.Lee
Wm. T., 9 June, 1876 (M W alive Lee)
    s/o Wm. M. Treadway & Frances Brisco
    par. b. Ows. & Hanc. Co., TN; R.Lee
TWYMAN
Leslie, 24 Aug., 1875 (M W alive Lee)
    s/o B[roaddus]. W. Twyman & Lucy Gale
    par. b. Woodford & Franklin; R.Lee
Sidney, 23 Oct., 1878 ("F" W alive Lee)
    s/o Broaddus W. Twyman & Lucy Gale
    par. b. Woodford & Franklin; R.Lee
TYLER
-----, 10 Oct., 1875 (M W alive Lee)
    s/o Charles D. Tyler & Mary E. Hill
    par. b. Lee Co., VA & Br.; R.Lee
    [appar. d. pre-1880]

VANDERPOOL
nn, 27 June, 1874 (M W dead Lee)
    s/o Isaac Vanderpool & Racheal Cooper
    par. b. Ows. & Floyd; R.Lee
    [Isaac & Rachel md. 6 Nov., 1873 Lee]
nn, 13 March, 1875 (F? W dead Lee)
    ch/o Isaac Vanderpool & Rachel Cooper
    par. b. Floyd & Ows.; R.Lee; twin
nn, 13 March, 1875 (F? W dead Lee)
    ch/o Isaac Vanderpool & Rachel Cooper
    par. b. Floyd & Ows.; R.Lee; twin
Amanda, 22 March, 1874 (F W alive Lee)
    d/o Abraham Vanderpool & Amanda Estes
    par. b. Scott Co., VA & Est.; R.Lee
America, 28 April, 1878 (F W alive Lee)
    d/o Enoch Vanderpool & Delitha McLure
    par. b. Lee & Br.; R.Lee
    [Enoch & Delitha md. 21 Jan., 1875 Lee]

VANDERPOOL (cont.)

Elbert, 10 Jan., 1875 (M W alive Lee)
    s/o McKinley MALONEY & Therisa Vanderpool
    par. b. Ows. & Ows.; R.Lee; illegitimate
George Ella, 6 June, 1878 (F W alive Lee)
    d/o Isaac Vanderpool & Rachel Cooper
    par. b. Floyd & Ows.; R.Lee
Ibzan, 18 March, 1876 (M W alive Lee)
    s/o Isaac Vanderpool & Rachel Cooper
    par. b. Floyd & Ows.; R.Lee
Paulina F., 12 Oct., 1878 (F W alive Lee)
    d/o Wm. F. Vanderpool & Udocia W. Arnold
    par. b. Ows. & Lee Co., VA; R.Lee
Wm. L., 30 April, 1876 (M W alive Lee)
    s/o Enoch Vanderpool & Delitha McClure
    par. b. Ows. & Per.; R.Lee

WARD

Geo. W., 19 Oct., 1875 (M W alive Lee)
    s/o Ota H. Ward & Mary A. Sulavan
    par. b. Franklin Co, VA & Franklin Co, KY;
    R.Lee   [Ota & Mary md. 29 Aug., 1870 Lee]

WATSON

Manda, 9 July, 1878 (F W alive Lee)
    d/o Boone D. Watson & Rebecca Horn
    par. b. IN & Est.; R.Lee
William, 24 Feb., 1876 (M W alive Lee)
    s/o Daniel B[oone] Watson & Rebecca Horn
    par. b. IN & Est.; R.Lee

WEBB

James D., 15 Aug., 1876 (M W alive Lee)
    s/o Josiah Webb & Martha "Abney"
    par. b. Est. & Est.; R.Lee
Mervin, 15 June, 1878 (M W alive Lee)
    s/o Josiah Webb & Martha Abner
    par. b. Est. & Est.; R.Lee

WHISMAN

Enoch W., 10 Nov., 1878 (M W alive Lee)
    s/o Moses Whisman & Gilly Ann Stamper
    par. b. Br. & Br.; R.Lee
Rosanah, 4 Nov., 1878 (F W alive Lee)
    d/o Job L. Whisman & Barbara Shepard
    par. b. Scott Co., VA & Morg.; R.Lee

WHITE
Drucilla, 15 Dec., 1874 (F W alive Lee)
    d/o James White & America Roberts
    par. b. Mad. & Wlf.; R.Lee
    [tombstone reads b. 15 Jan., 1874,
    d. 25 Aug., 1965 - RCB]
Fred, 15 Aug., 1878 (M W alive Lee)
    s/o James White & America Roberts
    par. b. Mad. & Lee Co., VA; R.Lee
WILLIAMS
Edgar E. S., 5 Sept., 1878 (M W alive Lee)
    s/o John W. F. Williams & Alice "G" Shearer
    par. b. Ows. & Ows.; R.Lee
Frederic V. R., 20 Nov., 1876 (M W alive Lee)
    s/o John W. F. Williams & Alice C. Shearer
    par. b. Ows. & Ows.; R.Lee
Lory E[llen], 22 Dec., 1875 (F W alive Lee)
    d/o Noah Williams & Eliza A. Hobbs
    par. b. Per. & Wlf.; R.Lee
Million, 2 Oct., 1875 (F W alive Lee)
    d/o Andrew Williams & Sally Puckett
    par. b. Per. & Br.; R.Lee
WILSON
Alice, 5 June, 1878 (F W alive Lee)
    d/o David Wilson & Mary J[ane] Gabbard [see
    mgs.]; par. b. Ows. & Br.; R.Lee
WOODEN
Thomas S., 22 Sept., 1878 (M Blk alive Lee)
    s/o Geo. R. Wooden & Rachel Smith
    par. b. Ows. & Let.; R.Lee
WRIGHT
-----, 17 June, 1874 (M W dead Lee)
    s/o Thos. A. Wright & "Louisa" Dixon
    par. b. Marion Co, MO & Aberdeen, OH; R.Lee
    [Thos. & "Lucella" md. 14 March, 1873 Lee]
nn, 10 Dec., 1874 (M W alive Lee)
    s/o Lewis H. Wright & Susan Maloney
    par. b. Ows. & Ows.; R.Lee
Claude, 22 Jan., 1878 (M W alive Lee)
    s/o Thomas Wright & "Loula" Dixon
    par. b. Madison Co., MO & Brown Co., OH;
    R.Lee [apparently twin of Maud; see deaths]
Martha E., 18 Nov., 1878 (F W alive Lee)
    d/o Marshall M. Wright & Eliz. J. Nichols
    par. b. Ows. & Wlf.; R.Lee

WRIGHT (cont.)
Maud, 22 Jan., 1878 (F W alive Lee)
    d/o Thomas Wright & "Loula" Dixon
    par. b. Madison Co., MO & Brown Co., OH;
    R.Lee [apparently twin of Claude]
Robert, 24 July, 1875 (M W alive Lee)
    s/o Thos. A. Wright & "Luella" Dixon
    par. b. Marion Co., MO & Aberdeen, OH;
    R.Lee
WYATT
Deller, 4 June, 1878 (F W alive Lee)
    d/o Geo. B. Wyatt & Mary P. Turley [see
    mgs.]; par. b. Est. & Ows.; R.Lee
    [Deller appar. d. pre-1880]

YORK
Alfred, 24 March, 1874 (M W alive Lee)
    s/o Wm. York & Ellen Ketcham
    par. b. Ows. & Br.; R.Lee
John S. C., 11 March, 1878 (M W alive Lee)
    s/o Wm. York & Ellen Ketcham
    par. b. Ows. & Br.; R.Lee
Wm. D., 7 April, 1876 (M W alive Lee)
    s/o Wm. J. York & Ellen Ketcham
    par. b. Ows. & Br.; R.Lee

40

DEATH RECORDS - 1874-1878

ABNER
Pheba C. (F W S; 5 mos.) d. 18 July, 1876
    cause uk.; b.Lee; R.Lee; d.Lee
    d/o Louis & Amelia Ann Abner [nee Gum], b.
    KY & KY
ANGEL
James (M W S; 9) d. 20 March, 1878, killed by
    a horse; b.Lee; R.Lee; d.Lee
    s/o Andrew & Malvin Angel [nee Gross],
    b. KY & KY
Malvin (F W md; 29; Hkpr.) d. 1 Aug., 1878 of
    a cold; b.Br.; R.Lee; d.Lee
    d/o Henry & Louisa Gross, b. KY & KY
    [wf/o Andrew Angel]
ASHCRAFT
Algernon (M W S; 2 mos) d. 29 Feb, 1874 [1875]
    of Quinsy; b.Lee; R.Lee; d.Lee;
    s/o Wm. & Hannah Ashcraft [nee Wilson], b.
    Ows & Lee Co, VA [NOTE: He was b. 12/74,
    so he must have d. in 1875, not 1874]

BAKER
Margaret A. (F W S; 7 mos.) d. 19 Oct, 1876 of
    inflamation of brain; b.Lee; R.Lee; d.Lee;
    d/o John W. & Mary A. Baker, b. NC & KY
BARRETT
Elizabeth (F W S; 26) d. 15 Nov., 1875 of
    consumption; b.Br.; R.Lee; d.Lee;
    d/o Isom & Eliza Barrett [nee Gross], b. KY
    & KY

41

BARRETT (cont.)
John (M W md.; 33; frm) d. 11 April, 1874 of
    typhus fever; b.Br.; R.Lee; d.Lee
    s/o James & Matilda Barrett [nee Stamper],
    b. Buncomb [Co.], NC & OH
Rebecca A. (F W S; 11 mo.) d. 25 Oct., 1875
    cause uk; b.Lee; R.Lee; d.Lee
    d/o Harrison & Louisa Barrett [Levisa nee
    Couch], b. KY & KY
    [listed as "Rosa Ann" in births]
BEACH
Samuel (M W S; 2 mo.) d. 18 April, 1878 of
    ----; b.Lee; R.Lee; d.Lee
    s/o C[lifton] M. & Lizza Beach, b. WV & KY
BEATTY
Caroline (F W md.; 32) d. 9 April, 1877 in
    childbirth; b.Ows.; R.Lee; d.Lee
    d/o James & Evaline McGUIRE [nee Trimble],
    b. KY & KY [wf/o James M. Beatty]
BEGLEY
Geo. (M W S; 7) d. 29 Jan., 1878 of Dyptheria;
    b.Lee; R.Lee; d.Lee
    s/o Swinfield & Mary Begley [nee Davidson],
    b. KY & KY
Martin (M W S; 12 mo.) d. - Sept., 1878 of
    croup; b.Laurel; R.Lee; d.Lee
    s/o James G. & Adaline Begley, b. MO & KY
BRANDENBURG
Martha (F W md.; 48) d. 14 Oct., 1877 of
    consumption; b.Est; R.Lee; d.Lee
    d/o Aquilla & Sally WHITE, b. KY & KY
    [appar. wf/o Jno.]

CHAMBERS
Robt. (M W S; 23; frm) d. 27 Sept, 1877 of
    Typhoid fever; b.Morg.; R.Lee; d.Lee
    s/o Wm. & Rebecca Chambers, b. Morg. & Clay
CHILDERS
Jane (F W S; 8 yrs, 6mo.) d. 21 Sept., 1875 of
    fever; b. John.; R.Lee; d.Boonevl.
    d/o W. H. & Mary J. Childers, b. VA & KY
COLE
Ostin [Austin] C (M W S; 28) d. 14 March, 1878
    of consumption; b.Ows.; R.Ows.; d.Lee
    s/o Ostin C & Paulina Cole, b. Bourb. & Est

COLE (cont.)
Rhoda A. (F W md.; 28) d. 10 Oct., 1874 of
    scrofula; b.Ows.; R.Lee; d.Lee
    d/o B. F. & Susan PHILLIPS, b. VA & Est.
    [wf/o Thomas Cole]
Susan (F W S; 18 mo.) d. 20 June, 1875 of
    Scrofula; b.Lee; R.Lee; d.Lee
    d/o Thos. & Rhoda Cole, b. KY & KY
CONGLETON
Ada (F W S; 6 days) d. 30 May, 1878 of
    inflamation of Bowells; b.Lee; R.Lee; d.Lee
    d/o Isaac & Paulina Congleton [nee Asbell],
    b. Ows & Ows
COOMER
Crittenden (F --? md.; 25; frm) d. 4 Oct, 1878
    of inflamation of bowells; b.Jack.; R.Lee;
    d.Lee;
    d/o Martha HOLLINGSWORTH, b. -----
James G. (M W S; 1 mo.) d. 24 Sept., 1877 of
    spinal affection; b.Lee; R.Lee; d.Lee
    s/o David & Nanna Coomer [nee Lucas], b. VA
    & VA
Jesse (M W S; 2) d. 1 Nov., 1874 of croup;
    b.Lee; R.Lee; d.Lee
    s/o Taylor & Martha Coomer; b. Lee Co., VA
    & --
CORNETT
Martha (F W "md"; 30) d. - May, 1877 of
    consumption; b.Lee Co., VA; R.Lee; d.Lee
    d/o Eli & Jane Cornett, b. VA & VA
    [a/L as Martha ROSS - see later]
CORUM
Daniel (M W S; 15; frm) d. 28 Sept., 1875 of
    typhoid fever; b.Ows; R.Lee; b.Lee
    s/o Wm. & Paulina Corum, b. KY & KY
COUCH
Elijah (M W md.; 65; frm) d. 1 Nov, 1874 of
    dropsy; b.Clay; R.Lee; d.Lee
    s/o John & Nancy Couch, b. uk & uk
CRABTREE
Jacob (M W md.; 78; frm) d. 19 June, 1877 of
    gravel; b.Lee Co., VA; R.Lee; d.Lee
    s/o Job & Rebecca Crabtree, b. VA & VA
Rosa B. (F W S; 6) d. ----- 1875 of spasms;
    b.Est.; R.Lee; d.Lee
    d/o Geo. A. & Eliza Crabtree [nee Rogers],
    b. VA & KY

43

CRAWFORD
Dilla A. (F W S; 1 yr, -? mo) d. 21 Sept, 1876
    of Dyptheria; b.Lee; R.Lee; d.Lee
    d/o Marcus & Letha Crawford [nee Fowler],
    b. KY & KY
James M. (M W S; 1 yr, 7 mo.) d. 29 Sept, 1876
    of croup; b.Lee; R.Lee; d.Lee
    s/o Wm. H. & Emily Crawford, b. KY & MO
Susannah (F W S; 6 mos.) d. 24 March, 1875 of
    brain fever; b.Lee; R.Lee; d.Lee
    d/o James & America Crawford [nee Plummer],
    b. KY & KY
CURRY
Andrew M. (M W md.; 28; frm) d. - Aug., 1874
    of --------?; b.Grayson Co, VA; R.Lee; d.Lee
    s/o Wm. & Ellen Curry, b. VA & uk

DAMRELL
Phoeba J. (F W S; 4) d. 19 March, 1878 of ----
    b.Lee; R.Lee; d.Lee
    d/o Joel & Phoeba Damrell [nee Wright], b.
    KY & KY
DAVIS
George Ann (F W md.; 24; Hkpr) d. 12 Aug, 1878
    of fever; b.Glasgow, MO; R.Lee; d.Lee
    d/o James & Matilda DUFF, b. VA & Mad.
    [wf/o James Davis]
DICKERSON
Edw. L. (M W S; 1 yr, 5 mo.) d. 6 Sept., 1876
    of Croup; b.Lee; R.Lee; d.Lee
    s/o James & Emily Dickerson, b. VA & KY
DOUGHERTY
Mallie M. (F W S; 5) d. 4 Jan., 1878 of
    Dyptheria; b.Lee; R.Lee; d.Lee
    d/o Frank & Martitia Dougherty [nee Cole];
    b. Ire. & KY
DUNAWAY
Eliz. (F W md.; 42) d. 6 July, 1877 of
    consumption; b.Lee Co., VA; R.Lee; d.Lee
    d/o Isaac & Nancy DUNAGIN, b. NC & NC
Priscilla (F W md.; 68; Hkpr.) d. 6 July, 1875
    of gravel; b.Lee; R.Lee; d.Lee
    d/o James & Didema McGUIRE [nee Mann], b.
    VA & VA [wf/o David W. Dunaway]
Thomas (M W md.; 42; frm) d. 28 Aug., 1875 of
    typhoid fever; b.Est; R.Lee; d.Lee
    s/o Benj. & Spicy Dunaway, b. KY & KY

DUNAWAY (cont.)
nn [William] (M W S; 3 days) d. 19 March, 1874
    cause uk; b.Lee; R.Lee; d.Lee
    s/o Wm. & Quintilla Dunaway [nee Estes], b.
    Ows. & Est.
DURBIN
Mary Ann (F W md.; 46; frm) d. 13 April, 1878
    of consumption; b.Est.; R.Lee; d.Lee
    d/o Clem & Nancy HOWARD, b. Mad. & Mad.
Nancy M. (F W S; 15; none) d. 19 Dec., 1874,
    burned; b.Ows; R.Lee; d.Lee
    d/o Jos. & Zerilda Durbin, b. Est. & Est.
    [NOTE: Nancy is only age 2 in the 1870
    census; her age s/b "6" @ time of death]
Wm. (M W S; 19; frm) d. - March, 1877 of sun
    stroke; b.Ows; R.Mad.; d.Lee
    s/o John & Sally Durbin, b.Est & Rockc.

FARMER
Matild[a] (F W md.; 38) d. 29 July, 1874 of
    fever; b.MO; R.Lee; d.Lee
    d/o Jos. & Nancy BRANDENBURG, b. uk
    [wf/o James F. - RMT]
FIELDS
Lona (F W md.; 32; Hkpr.) d. 30 Aug., 1876 of
    Inflamation of Spinal "chord"; b.Lee; R.Lee
    d.Lee; d/o --------
W. H. H. (M W md; 34; frm) d. 30 July, 1876 of
    Hemorhage of lungs; b.Lee; R.Lee; d.Lee
    s/o ---------
FLANNERY
Rachel (F W S; 8) d. Oct., 1877 of Dyptheria;
    b.Lee; R.Lee; d.Lee
    d/o Spencer & Eliz. Flannery, b. VA & KY
    [a/L as d. 24 Oct., 1878 of "soar" throat,
    age 9; par. b. KY & KY]
Wm. H. (M W S; 4) d. Oct., 1877 of Dyptheria;
    b.Lee; R.Lee; d.Lee
    s/o Spencer & Eliz. Flannery, b. VA & Ows.
    [a/L as d. 17 Nov., 1878 of "soar" throat,
    age 5; par. b. KY & KY]
FREY
Eliz. (F W wd.; 38) d. 25 Dec., 1878 of
    consumption; b.Ows; R.Lee; d.Lee
    d/o John A. & Pauline DUNAWAY, b. KY & KY

GILBERT
Letcher (M W S; 10 mo.) d. 17 Aug., 1878 of
    Diarhera; b.Lee; R.Lee; d.Lee
    s/o "Michle" [Michael?] & Sally Gilbert,
    b. KY & KY
Wm. H. (M W S; 2) d. 10 Oct., 1877 of disease
    of the liver; b.Lee; R.Lee; d.Lee
    s/o Francis & Phoeba Gilbert, b. Ows. &
    Scott Co, VA
GILLUM
Annabell (F W S; 13) d. 19 Aug., 1878 of
    coler(?) infantine; b.Knox; R.Lee; d.Lee
    d/o Marion & Sarah Gilum, b. Scott & Knox
GRAY
Benj. T. (M W md; 43; frm) d. 23 Oct., 1875
    of affected lungs; b.Lex.; R.Lee; d.Boonevl
    s/o Phillip SPUR, b. VA & VA
GUM
Mary J. (F W S; 15; frm) d. 8 Sept., 1878 of
    scarlet fever; b.Lee; R.Lee; d.Lee
    d/o Greenberry & Nancy Gum, b. Est. & VA

HALE
Wm. Jr. (M W S; 4) d. - Dec., 1877 of croupe;
    b.Lee; R.Lee; d.Lee
    s/o Wm. & Nancy Hale, b. VA & VA
HALL
Permelia (F W S; 7 mo; nothing) d 20 Oct, 1875
    of fever; b.Lee; R.Lee; d.Lee
    d/o Harvey & Sarah Hall [nee Thomas], b. KY
    & KY
HIERONYMOUS
Geo. (M W S; 3) d. 22 July, 1877 of fever
    b.Lee; R.Lee; d.Lee
    s/o Thos. & Margaret Hieronymous [nee Bush]
    b. KY & KY
HOBBS
Isaac S. (M W S; 5 mo.) d. 10 May, 1874 of
    croup; b.Lee; R.Lee; d.Lee
    s/o Wm. E. & Sarah Hobbs [nee Shoemaker],
    b. Lee Co, VA & Wlf.
HOLLAND
Chaney (F Blk md; 38) d. 26 Oct., 1877 of
    consumption; b.Let.; R.Lee; d.Lee
    d/o Tempa HOLBROOK, par. b. -- & KY
    [wf/o Tarlton Holland; listed as "Hampton"
    in births; Tarlton remd. pre-1880 census]

46

HORN

Manda (F W S; 3) d. 14 Feb., 1878 of brain
    fever; b.Lee; R.Lee; d.Est.
    d/o Aron & Suzan J. Horn, b. Est. & Ows.

HOUNSHELL

Milly A. (F W S; 8 mos.) d. 6 Jan., 1876 of
    fever; b.Lee; R.Lee; d.Lee
    d/o Frank & Judah Hounshell [nee Slone],
    b. VA & KY

HOWELL

Margaret Ann (F W S; 11; frm) d. 30 Sept, 1878
    of ----; b.Lee; R.Lee; d.Lee
    d/o Saml. P. & Eliza J Howell [nee Tincher]
    b. Est. & Ows.

HURLEY

John J. (M W S; 5) d. - Aug., 1876 of Dropsy;
    b.KY; R.Lee; d.Lee
    s/o John & Mary Hurley, b. TN & KY

JOHNSON

Amelia (F W S; 1 yr.) d. 17 Sept., 1876 of
    Typhoid fever; b.Lee; R.Lee; d.Lee
    d/o David & Mary Johnson, b. VA & NC
Anna F. (F W S; 10) d. 14 July, 1876 of
    Typhoid fever; b.Lee; R.Lee; d.Lee
    d/o David & Mary Johnson, b. VA & NC

JONES

Derias (M W S; 16; frm) d. 6 March, 1874 from
    boiler explosion; b.Floyd Co., VA; R.Lee;
    d.Lee
    s/o Joshua & Eunice Jones, b. Floyd Co, VA
    & Floyd Co., VA
John T. (M W S; 5 mos.) d. 18 Aug., 1876 of
    Scrofula; b.Lee; R.Lee; d.Lee
    s/o Stephen M. & Mary Jones [nee Tipton],
    b. VA & KY

JUDD

Biddy A. (F W S; 3) d. 12 Nov., 1877 of
    Dyptheria; b.Lee; R.Lee; d.Lee
    d/o James R. & Nancy Judd [nee Palmer], b.
    KY & KY [listed in births as "Lilly Ann"]
Martha B. (F W S; 1 yr.) d. 25 Dec., 1877 of
    Dyptheria; b.Lee; R.Lee; d.Lee
    d/o James R. & Nancy Judd [nee Palmer], b.
    KY & KY

KELLY
Henderson (M W S; 3) d. - April, 1877 of worms
    b.Lee; R.Lee; d.Lee
    s/o Speed C. & Margaret Kelly [nee Smyth],
    b. KY & KY
KIDD
Wm. H. (M W S; 3 mos.) d. - June, 1874 of
    Measles; b.Lee; R.Lee; d.Lee
    s/o Samuel & Elvira Kidd [nee King], b. Br.
    & Br.
KINCAID
George B. (M W md; 59; mech) d. 16 April, 1875
    killed by falling tree; b.Est; R.Lee; d.Lee
    s/o Peggy & Geo. Kincaid, b. uk & uk
KING
Alwilda (F W S; 9 mos.) d. 10 Aug., 1877 of
    croupe; b.Lee; R.Lee; d.Lee
    d/o Adison & "Alwilda" King [nee Tolby], b.
    KY & KY

LUCAS
James S. (M W S; 8 mos.) d. 5 June, 1878,
    cause uk.; b.Lee; R.Lee; d.Lee
    s/o Wm. B. & Lucinda Lucas, b. VA & TN
LUTES
Adda (F W S; 1 yr.) d. 12 Oct., 1874 of
    congestion of brain, suddenly; b.Lee;
    R.Lee; d.Lee
    d/o Christopher C. & Lucinda Lutes [nee
    Roberts], b. Est. & Est.

McGUIRE
Ansel D. (M W md; 49; frm) d. 7 Dec., 1875 of
    typhoid fever; b.Est.; R.Lee; d.Lee
    s/o Benj. & Didema McGuire [nee Mann],
    b. KY & KY
Catharine (F W md; 42) d. 12 May, 1877 of
    consumption; b.Est.; R.Lee; d.Lee
    d/o Wm. & Perdelia AKERS, b. KY & KY
    [wf/o John Warwick McGuire]

MALONEY
Wm. (M W md; 70; frm) d. 17 June, 1875 of
    carbuncle ulcer, b. Buncombe Co, NC; R.Lee;
    d.Lee
    s/o John & Susannah Maloney [nee Crawford],
    b. NC & NC

MANN

Martin (M W md; 56; frm) d. 4 July, 1877 of
    Scroffula; b.Est.; R.Lee; d.Lee
    s/o John & Patsy Mann [nee Tincher], b. KY
    & KY
Patsey (F W wd; 79) d. 2 Jan., 1878 of chills;
    b.Clk.; R.Clk.; d.Lee
    d/o Samuel & Esther TINCHER [mother was
    Priscilla, not Esther, nee Mann] b. VA & VA
    [wf/o John]

MARSHALL

Joannah (F W md; 35; Hwf.) d. 14 March, 1878
    of consumption; b.Per; R.Lee; d.Lee
    d/o Isaac & Mary SPENCER, b. VA & VA
    [wf/o Robert Marshall]

MAYS

Harvey (M W S; 3) d. - Oct., 1877 of
    Dyptheria; b.Lee; R.Lee; d.Lee
    s/o Andrew & Rachel Mays, b. KY & KY
    [listed as "Henry" in births]

MILLER

----- (M W S; 1 day) d. 15 Sept., 1878,
    L-----? of the mother; b.Lee; R.Lee; d.Lee
    s/o Josiah & Orrelia Miller [nee Johnson],
    b. KY & KY

NEWTON

Rauley (M W S; 4) d. - Oct, 1877 of Dyptheria;
    b.Lee; R.Lee; d.Lee
    s/o Wm. & Ella Newton, b. KY & KY

NOLEN

Sarah (F W md; 19) d. 26 March, 1877 of
    childbed fever; b.Ows; R.Lee; d.Lee
    d/o Francis M. & Clarinda SNOWDEN [nee
    Baker], b. Est. & VA
    [wf/o Lemuel Noland; see mgs.]

OLIVER

John R. (M W S; 6 days) d. 2 March, 1878 of
    -----; b.Lee; R.Lee; d.Lee
    s/o Geo. & Malvar Oliver [nee Chambers],
    b. Ows. & KY
    [NOTE: a/L same date 1877 as unnamed male,
    age 4 days; rest of data the same. The
    1878 date is correct - see births.]

PALMER
Elias (M W wd; 86; frm) d. 20 July, 1875 of
    gravel; b.Halifax Co., VA; R.Lee; d.Lee
    par. uk
PITMAN
Micajah (M W md; 63; mech.) d. 2 Jan, 1876 of
    intemperance; b.NC; R.Lee; d.Lee
    s/o (smeared, unreadable), b. ----
POWELL
Monroe (M W S; 24; frm) d. 10 Nov., 1874 of
    pneumonia fever; b.Lee Co, VA; R.Lee; d.Lee
    s/o John S. & Minerva Powell, b. Lee Co, VA
    & Taz. Co., VA
PRYSE
Nannie E. (F W S; 6) d. 6 Oct., 1875 of brain
    fever; b.Lee; R.Lee; d.Beattyville
    d/o David & Lucy A. Pryse, b. Wales & KY

ROBERTS
James (M W S; 4) d. 13 July, 1877 of pain in
    knee & leg; b.Lee; R.Lee; d.Lee
    s/o John & Eliz. Roberts, b. IA & Morg.
ROBINSON
John (M W S; 16; frm) d. 15 April, 1874 of gun
    shot; b.Wlf; R.Lee; d.Lee
    s/o John & Rhoda Robinson, b. VA & VA
ROSS
Herrod (M W md; 65; frm) d. 29 Feb, 1874 of
    measles; b.Mad.; R.Lee; d.Lee
    s/o Larry & Castora Ross, b. uk
James (M W S; 21; frm) d. 26 Oct, 1874 of
    measles; b.Ows.; R.Lee; d.Lee
    s/o Herrod & Vina Ross, b. Mad. & Clk.
Martha (F W md; 30) d. 9 May, 1877 of a cold;
    b.VA; R.Lee; d.Lee
    d/o Eli & Jane CORNETT, b. VA & VA
    [a/L as Martha Cornett]
Peter (M W S; 20; frm) d. 14 Oct, 1874 of
    measles; b.Ows.; R.Lee; d.Lee
    s/o Herrod & Vina Ross, b. Mad. & Clark

SCHOLL
Lawrence A. (M W S; 4) d. 13 May, 1878 of
    pulmonary consumption; b.Pow.; R.Lee; d.---
    s/o Wm. C. & Laura Scholl, b. KY & MO

SLONE
---- (M W S; 1 day) d. - Feb., 1877, cause uk;
    b.Lee; R.Lee; d.Lee
    s/o Nathan & Susan Slone, b. Floyd & VA
SMALLWOOD
Elias H. (M W S; 5) d. 23 Jan., 1876 of
    Dyptheria; b.Lee; R.Lee; d.Lee
    s/o David E[dmund] & Lucy Smallwood [nee
    Gorden], b. KY & KY
SMITH
----- (M W S; --) d. 7 Feb., 1878 of ------;
    b.Lee; R.Lee; d.Lee
    s/o Henry & Polly Smith [nee Roberts], b.
    KY & KY
Lucinda (F W md; 25) d. 24 Oct., 1874 of
    consumption; b.Let.; R.Lee; d.Lee
    d/o Robt. & Letta AMBURGH[Y], b. uk & Let.
Wiley (M W md; 28; frm) d. 25 July, 1874 of
    pistol shot; b. Harl.; R.Lee; d.Lee
    s/o Hugh Smith & mother uk, b. uk & --
SPARKS
Isaac (M W wd; 80; crptr.) d. 2 June, 1878 of
    dropsy; b.Clk.; R.Lee; d.Lee
    s/o Elisha Sparks & --------, b. ----
SPENCER
Martha (F W S; 5) d. 17 May, 1877 of pain in
    knee; b.Lee; R.Lee; d.Lee
    d/o John D. & Catharine Spencer [nee Hobbs]
    b. Br. & VA
STAMPER
Larkin (M W md; 62; frm) d. 18 Oct., 1875 of
    typhoid fever; b.NC; R.Lee; d.Lee
    s/o Joel & Mary Stamper, b. NC & NC
STRONG
Mary P. (F W S; 13) d. 29 Nov, 1874, cause uk;
    b.Br.; R.Lee; d.Lee
    d/o Alex. & Sarah Strong [nee Chambers], b.
    Br. & Morg.

THOMAS
Eleanor C[ath.] (F W md; 18) d. 21 Dec., 1875
    of childbed fever; b.Ows; R.Lee; d.Lee
    d/o Wm. & Polly THOMPSON, b. VA & VA
    [wf/o James M. Thomas - see mgs. & births]

THOMAS (cont.)
Jesse M. (F W S; 10 mos.) d. 14 Feb., 1876 of
    Scrofula; b.Beattyvl.; R.Lee; d.Lee
    s/o D[avid] S[ale] & Diadema Thomas [nee
    McGuire], b KY & KY
Varr (M W S; 3) d. 15 Oct., 1877 of Dyptheria;
    b.Lee; R.Lee; d.Lee
    s/o Henry H. & Jane Thomas [nee Shoemaker]
    b. KY & KY
Zachariah B. (M W S; 91; salt maker) d. 3 Feb,
    1876 of old age; b. VA; R.Lee; d.Lee
    s/o Jesse & Jane Thomas, b. VA & VA
TINCHER
Margaret (F W md; 73; frm) d. 4 June, 1878 of
    colic; b.Shelby; R.Lee; d.Lee
    d/o Randall & Rachel SMALLWOOD [nee
    Ashcraft], b. ---- [wf/o Wm. H. Tincher]

WADE
Hiram ("F" W S; 2) d. 2 Oct., 1877 of
    Dyptheria; b.Lee; R.Lee; d.Lee
    s/o Ira & Cely Wade [nee Cornett], b. AL &
    VA
WELLS
Hettiller(?) (F Blk S; 2) d. 20 Sept., 1878 of
    brain fever; b.Lee; R.Lee; d.Lee
    d/o John M. & Mary Wells, b. KY & KY
WILLIAMS
George (M W S; 11; frm) d. 26 Jan., 1874 of
    disease of the spine; b.Ows; R.Lee; d.Lee
    s/o Geo. & Everine Williams, b.Culpeper, VA
    & Est.
WRIGHT
Claude (M W S; age one-half) d. 23 July, 1878
    of Chronic Diahrea; b.Lee; R.Lee; d.Lee
    s/o Thomas A. & Louella Wright [nee Dixon],
    b. MO & OH

MARRIAGE RECORDS - 1874-1878

ABNER
JOHN (Lee 32 S frm b.Ows.) par. b. VA & VA
    SARAH E[llen] LUTES (Lee 23 S b.Ows.)
    par. b. Est. & Est.
    [d/o Chas. Lutes & Lucinda Plummer]
    8 Dec., 1878 Lee [a/L 8 Nov. Lee Mgs.]
ANGEL
JULIUS (Lee 23 S frm b.KY); par. b. ----
    [s/o Ephraim & Susan Angel]
    LUCY J. BRANDENBURG (Lee 17 S b.KY) KY & KY
    4 Aug., 1876 Lee [a/L 1877 Lee Mgs.]
ARNOLD
GEO. W. (Lee 24 S frm b.TN)
    s/o L[orenzo] D. & Polly Arnold
    MARY THOMAS (Lee 21 S b.Ows.)
    d/o James & Mary H. Thomas
    8 Jan., 1874, Lee
ASBELL
SAMUEL (Lee 24 S frm b.Ows.)
    s/o H[enry] B. Asbell & --- [Eliza Johnson]
    MARY E. GERLEY (Lee 19 S b.Claiborne, TN)
    d/o J. C. & Lucinda Gerley
    1 April, 1874, Lee
ASHCRAFT
WILLIAM (Lee 29 S frm b.Ows.)
    s/o Jas. & Eliz. Ashcraft [nee McCullum]RWO
    HANNAH WILSON (Lee 18 S b.Lee Co., VA)
    d/o A. & Mary Wilson
    5 March, 1874, Lee

BEACH
C[lifton]. M. (Beattyvl. 37 S shoemaker b.VA)
    par. b. -----
    LIZZIE CRAWFORD (Lee 26 S b.KY) KY & KY
    2 Sept., 1875, Lee
BEATTY
THOMAS (Est. 23 S frm b.KY) par. b. KY & KY
    LUCY LIGHTFOOT (Lee 18 S b.KY) par. KY & KY
    26 April, 1877, Lee
BOLAN (BOWLING)
KEEN (Jack. 28 2nd frm b.Br.) Lee, VA & Br.
    MARTHA J. FARMER (Jack. 17 S b.KY) par. b.
    Scott Co., VA & KY
    md. 19 March, 1879   [NOTE: The other mgs.
    on this page were 1878]
BOOTH
GEO. W. (Fleming 21 S frm b.KY) par. VA & VA
    [s/o John Booth & Nancy Spencer - BOws]
    SARAH BELOMY (Lee 19 S b.VA) par. TN & VA
    11 Feb., 1877, Lee
BOWLING
(see BOLAN)
BRANDENBURGH
S[amuel] P. (Lee 30 S frm b.Ows.)
    s/o Jno. & Debora Brandenburgh
    MARY C. SMITH (Lee 18 S b.Ows.)
    d/o Henry & Jane Smith
    22 Oct., 1874, Lee
BROWN
JAMES (Lee 37 S frm b.VA) par. b. VA & VA
    LOURENIA MADDIX (Lee 17 S b.Br.) par. b.
    Lee Co., VA & Lee
    27 June, 1878, Lee   [Blk - per births]
BURK
GEO. P. (Lee 27 S mcht. b.KY) par. b. VA & VA
    VIVIA McGUIRE (Lee 20 S b.KY) par. KY & VA
    [d/o Wm. McGuire & Rebecca Blount]
    27 Sept., 1877, Lee

CALDWELL
WM. S. (Lee 21 S frm b.Lee) par. NC & Lee, VA
    [s/o Freeland H. Caldwell & Eliz. Shoemaker
    - BOws.]
    LOUISA SMITH (Est. 17 S b.Est.) par. b. Lee
    Co., VA & Lee Co., VA
    31 Dec., [1878], Est.

CHARLES
FRANK (Est. 23 S frm b.KY) par. b. ----
    NANCY TOWNSEND (Lee 18 S b.KY) par. KY & KY
    18 June, 1876, Lee [8 June per Lee mgs.]
COCKERHAM/COCKRUM
ZACHARY T[aylor] (Lee 22 S frm b.KY) VA & KY
    [s/o James Cockrum & Sarah Wright - BOws.]
    MARGRET LUTES (Lee 14 S b.KY) par. KY & VA
    [d/o James & Caroline Lutes]
    16 Aug., 1877, Lee
COLE
W[m.] H. (Lee 27 S frm b.KY) par. b. KY & KY
    NANNIE E. STEEL (Lee 19 S b.KY) par.NC & KY
    17 April, 1877, Lee
COOMER
RILEY (Lee 22 S frm b.Lee Co., VA)
    s/o T. & Sally Coomer
    LURANIA KILBURN (Lee 17 S b.Br.)
    d/o O. Crawford & Matilda Kilburn
    6 Nov., 1874, Lee
COOPER
ALFRED (Lee 23 S frm b. uk & uk
    MARTHA E[LLEN] COLE (Lee 21 S b.KY) NC & KY
    24 July, 1875, Lee [a/L 28 July, Lee Mgs]
COUCH
ELI (Lee 19 S frm b.KY) par. b. KY & KY
    [s/o Enoch Couch & Ursula A. Bishop - BOws]
    EMILY [JANE] MANN (Lee 19 S b.KY) KY & KY
    [d/o Martin Mann & Mary J. Hall - BOws.]
    10 Sept., 1876, Lee
CREECH
HENRY (Lee 21 S frm b.KY) par. b. KY & KY
    [s/o Elijah Creech & Nancy Brandenburg -
    BOws.]
    MARY F. BRANDENBURGH (Lee 19 S b.KY) par.
    b. KY & KY
    [d/o John Brandenburg & Patsy White - BOws]
    31 Aug., 1876, Lee [listed 1877, Lee Mgs.]

DAMERALL
FRANKLIN (Lee 24 S frm b.Br.)
    s/o Samuel & Sally Damerall
    ALLICE OVERBEE (Lee 19 S b.VA)
    d/o ------
    - Oct., 1874, Lee

55

DAVIES
R. H. (Lee 35 2nd sch.tchr. b.VA) par. VA & VA
    RHODA E. BEATTY (Lee 29 S b.KY) par.KY & KY
    7 Dec., 1876, Lee
DEATON
ALFRED (Lee 22 S frm b.KY) par. b. IN & VA
    [s/o John Deaton & Rebecca Lucas]
    ALWILDA KING (Lee 15 S b.Wlf) Clay & Est.
    [d/o Jeremiah & Eliz. King]
    19 Sept, 1875, Lee [a/L 23 Sept, Lee Mgs.]
DICKERSON
JAS. W. (Lee 24 S frm b.Charlotte, VA)
    s/o Jno. J. & Matilda Dickerson
    EMILY WHITE (Lee 23 S b.Mad.)
    d/o B. F[ranklin] & Sally White
    10 June, 1874, Lee
DUKE
JOSEPH (Lee 22 S frm b.Ows.) par. b. TN & Est.
    LUCIN[DA] DURBIN (Lee 16 S b.Mad) Ows & Est
    [d/o Edward Durbin & Patience Lynch]
    2 Aug., [1878]
DUNAWAY
JOHN (Lee 19 S frm b.KY) par. b. KY & VA
    [s/o Thos. Dunaway & Eliz. Dunagin? - BOws]
    MARY MARSHALL (Lee 19 S b.KY) par. NC & VA
    [d/o Wm. Marshall & Sarah Thompson - BOws.]
    20 Dec., 1877, Lee
DURBIN
JOHN M. (Lee 23 S frm b.KY) par. b. KY & KY
    [s/o Joseph & Surilla Durbin - BOws.]
    EVALINE WARNER (Lee 18 S b.KY) par. KY & KY
    7 July, 1877, Lee

ELLIOTT
DAWSON (Est. 26 S frm b.KY) par. b. KY & KY
    BETHENA SLONE (Lee 18 S b.KY) par. KY & KY
    15 Sept., 1876, Lee
ESTES
HENRY (Lee 23 S frm b.KY) par. b. KY & KY
    [s/o Fielding Estes & Emily Jane Estes]
    MARGARET NEWMAN (Lee 17 S b.KY) par.KY & KY
    16 July, 1876, Lee
    [listed 27 July, 1877, Lee Mgs.]
WILLIAM (Lee 18 S frm b.Est.) par. Pow. & Est.
    [s/o Fielding Estes & Emily Jane Estes]
    LAURA ESTES (Lee 17 S b.Br.) par. b. -----
    27 Dec., 1878 [listed 28 Nov., Lee Mgs.]

56

EVANS
JESSE (Ows. 22 S frm b.KY) par. b. KY & KY
    [s/o Hiram Evans & Polly Stamper - BOws.]
    ELIZABETH HALL (Lee 18 S b.KY) par. VA & KY
    14 June, 1877, Lee [a/L 19 June, Lee Mgs.]

FARMER
SIMPSON L. (Lee uk S frm b.--) [age 22 per Lee
    Mgs.] par. b. -- & KY
    JOANAH BLACKWELL (Lee 16 S b.Est) Est & Est
    15 Oct., 1878
FIKE
JOSEPH (Lee 25 S frm b.KY) par. Germ. & KY
    LUCINDA BURNES(?) (Lee 21 S b.KY) KY & KY
    - April, 1875, Lee [a/L 8 May, Lee Mgs.]
FORTNER (listed 1880 census as FAULKNER)
GEO. A. (Lee 21 S frm b.KY) par. b. -- & KY
    MARGRET A. WEILER (Lee 16 S b.KY) par. b.
    Germ. & KY
    22 April, 1877, Lee

GABBARD
JOHN (Lee 21 S frm b.KY) par. b. KY & KY
    [s/o Geo. Gabbard - BOws.]
    LYDIA A[NN] CHAMBERS (Lee 20 S b.KY) par.
    b. KY & KY
    16 Dec., 1875, Lee
GARLAND
PRIOR (Lee 22 2nd frm b.TN)
    s/o Prior & Margaret Garland
    REBECA BARRETT (Lee 22 S b.Br.)
    d/o Jas. & Matilda Barrett [nee Stamper]
    24 Dec., 1874, Lee

HADDIX
RUBEN (Wlf. 23 S frm b.KY) par. b. KY & KY
    POLLY A[NN] JOHNSON (Lee 15 S b.KY) KY & KY
    10 May, 1877, Lee
HALEY
AUSTIN (Lee 23 S frm b.Ows.)
    s/o Jas. & ----? Haley [Ninnie per 1870
    census]
    MARY MADOX (Lee 16 S b.Ows.)
    d/o -------- & Martha Madox
    12 Aug., 1874, Lee [Blk per births]

HALL
JOHN C. (Lee 20 S frm b.KY) par. b. VA & KY
    LUCY ANN TINCHER (Lee 19 S b.KY) KY & KY
    [d/o Jas. Tincher & Susannah Gordon - BOws]
    16 Dec., 1877, Lee
HAMMAN
PHILIP (Beattyvl, Lee 47 S miller b.Montg.)
    s/o J[ames] L. & Susan Hamman
    PHEBE J[ANE] STAMPER (Lee 32 S b.Br.)
    d/o J[ohn] A. & Lucinda Stamper [nee Kash]
    12 July, 1874, Lee
HORN
WM. (Lee 21 S frm b.KY) par. b. KY & KY
    MARY J[ANE] PIGG (Lee 16 S b.KY) KY & KY
    - July, 1876, Lee
    [listed 6 July, 1877 Lee Mgs.]
HOWARD
SAMUEL (Lee 26 S frm b.Br.) par. Harl. & Ows.
    MALINDA J. BAILEY (Lee 29 2nd b.Br.) par.
    b. Harl. & Br.
    6 June, 1878
HOWERTON
ALBERT G. (Lee 34 2nd lab. b.KY) par. VA & KY
    AUGUSTY BURGER (Lee 22 S b.NC) Germ. & KY
    20 Nov., 1877, Lee
HUGHES
E[DWARD] D. (Lee 25 S. sch.tchr. b.KY) KY & KY
    SUSAN P. ROBERTS (Lee 16 S b.KY) VA & TN
    17 July, 1877, Lee

JOHNSON
JOHN (Lee 19 S frm b.Ows.)
    s/o Timothy & Sally Johnson [nee Pitman]
    LUCINDA SLONE (Lee 17 S b.Ows.)
    d/o Jesse & Eliza Slone
    - Oct., 1874, Lee [a/L 26 Oct., Lee Mgs.]
WASHINGTON (Lee 38 2nd frm b.VA) par. VA & VA
    MARY JOHNSON (Lee 26 2nd b.KY) par. KY & KY
    14 June, 1877, Lee

KENDRICK
JAMES B. (Lee 24 S frm b.KY) par. b. VA & NC
    MARGRET THOMAS (Lee 21 S b. KY) par.VA & KY
    3 Feb., 1877, Lee [a/L 4 Feb., Lee Mgs.]

KETCHUM
JEREMIAH (Lee 30 2nd miner b.KY) par. KY & KY
    ANNA BENNETT (Lee 20 S b.KY) par. MO & KY
    3 Sept., 1877, Lee
KINCAID
JAMES (Wlf. 19 S frm b.Ows.) par. Est. & Br.
    JOANNAH TYRA (Wlf. 18 S b.KY) par. KY & KY
    28 Feb., 1878
SAMUEL P[LUMMER] (Lee 19 S frm b.KY) KY & KY
    [s/o Socrates Kincaid & Cynthia Trimble]
    GILLY ANN COCKERHAM (Lee 20 S b.KY) VA & KY
    [d/o Jas. "Cockran" & Emily Stamper - BOws]
    10 May, 1877, Lee
KIRK
WM. G. (Lee 50 2nd mech. b.--) par. b. ---
    HALEY [MAHALA] WILLIAMS (Lee 22 S b.KY)
    par. b. KY & VA
    16 Aug., 1876, Lee

LEGG
ANDREW J. (Lee 20 S frm b.Lee Co, VA)
    s/o Jas. P. & Hannah Legg
    NARCISSA J[ANE] GUM (Lee 19 S b.Ows.)
    d/o W[m.] B. & Lucinda Gum [nee Benton]
    8 Jan., 1874, Lee
LUCAS
JAMES R[OBT.] (Lee 24 2nd frm b.VA) VA & VA
    CYNTHIAN OLINGER (Lee 20 S b.KY) VA & VA
    30 Aug., 1877, Lee
W[M]. T. (Lee 20 S frm b.KY) par. b. VA & VA
    MARY ANN PLUMMER (Lee 21 S b.KY) KY & KY
    4 Oct., 1877, Lee
LUTES
FRANCIS M. (Lee 21 S frm b.Ows) par. Est & Est
    [s/o Christopher Lutes & Lurinda Roberts -
    BOws.]
    NANCY E. KINCAID (Lee 16 S b.KY) par. b.
    Est. & Montg.
    22 Nov., 1878 KY
SAMUEL (Lee 24 S frm b.KY) par. b. KY & KY
    [s/o Charles Lutes & Lucinda Plummer]
    HARRIET A. BEATTY (Lee 23 S b.KY) KY & KY
    1 June, 1876, Lee

McLANE
ELBERT (Nicholas 26 S frm b.TN) par. b. ----
    REBECCA CABLE (Lee 28 S b.VA) par. TN & VA
    30 Dec., 1875, Lee

MALONEY
FRANKLIN P. (Lee 23 S frm b.KY) par. NC & IL
    [s/o Wm. Maloney & Permelia Rhodes]
    MARY E. WILLIS (Lee 17 S b.KY) par. TN & TN
    29 Nov., 1877, Lee
MARSHALL
[BENJ.] FRANKLIN (Lee 24 S frm b.Lee Co., VA)
    par. b. NC & VA
    [s/o Wm. Marshall & Sarah Thompson - BOws.]
    [MARY] ELIZABETH LUCAS (Lee 24 S b.VA)
    par. b. VA & VA
    25 July, 1878, Lee
MAYS
JACKSON (Lee 26 S frm b.KY) par. b. KY & KY
    JOAN [JOANNAH] ESTES (Lee 22 S b.KY) par.
    b. KY & KY
    6 Dec., 1877, Lee
METCALFE
JOSHUA (Ows. 21 S frm b.Est.) par. b. ---
    MARGARET MAZE (Lee 17 S b.Ows.) Per. & Est.
    8 June, 1878 [listed 9 June, Lee Mgs.]
MILLER
ELHANNON (Est 22 2nd frm b.Br.) par. Br. & Br.
    FLORENCE E. JOHNSON (Est. 16 S b.Wlf.) par.
    b. Montg. & Br.
    3 Jan., [1878], Est.
MORRIS
FRANCIS T. (Lee 22 S frm b.KY) par. b. NC & VA
    NANCY J. CHRISMAN (Lee 17 S b.KY) VA & VA
    9 Aug., 1877, Lee

NOLAND
LEMUEL (Lee 21 S frm b.KY) par. b. KY & KY
    SARAH SNOWDEN (Lee 17 S b.KY) par. KY & VA
    [d/o Francis M. Snowden & Clarinda Baker]
    19 Aug., 1875, Lee
LOUIS (Lee 21 S frm b.KY) par. b. KY & KY
    NANCY M. CURRY (Lee 23 2nd b.VA) VA & VA
    [listed as Nancy "Ann" in Lee Mgs.]
    28 May, 1876, Lee [a/L 29 May, Lee Mgs.]

NORMAN
OWEN (Lee 30 2nd frm b.KY) par. b. KY & --
    NANCY FIELDS (Lee 20 S b.KY) par. KY & KY
    [listed as "Minerva" Fields in Lee Mgs.]
    25 Dec., 1875, Lee

PHILLIPS
SILAS E. (Lee 41 S frm b.KY) par. b. VA & KY
    HESTER J[ANE] HENSLEY (Lee 38 2nd b.TN)
    par. b. TN & VA [a/L as "Hunter", Lee Mgs.]
    5 Aug., 1875, Lee
PORTER
LEWIS (Lee 22 S frm b.Ows.) par. b. -- & Est.
    SARAH NEWMAN (Lee 24 S b.Ows.) par. b.
    Clk. & Clk.
    31 Jan., 1878

REESE
JOHN (Lee 18 S frm b.KY) par. b. TN & TN
    [s/o Joseph Reece & Judah Brewer - BOws.]
    MARY E. MAYS (Lee 18 S b.KY) par. KY & KY
    20 Aug., 1876, Lee [a/L 23 Aug., Lee Mgs.]
ROGERS
JOHN A. (Est. 22 S frm b.KY) par. b. KY & KY
    MARIAM B. McINTIRE (Lee 14 S b.KY) KY & KY
    1 Nov., 1877, Lee

SHEARER
GEO. W. J. (Lee 24 S frm b.KY) par. b. KY & VA
    [s/o Albert Shearer & Narcissa Blount -
    BOws.]
    LAURA E. MALONEY (Lee 15 S b.KY) KY & KY
    [d/o John Maloney & Sally Ashcraft]
    19 July, 1877, Lee
SHEPARD
E[mmon] L. (Ows. 28 S preaching b.OH) OH & OH
    REBECCA C. JONES (Lee 26 S b.VA) VA & VA
    26 April, 1877, Lee
SHOEMAKER
HENRY (Lee 18 S frm b.Ows.)
    s/o E[lisha] & S[usannah] Shoemaker
    HASIAH WILLIAMS (Lee 20 S b.Per.)
    d/o A. & Sally Williams
    4 June, 1874, Lee

SLONE
SHADRIC (Lee 30 S frm b.Pike) par. Pike & Est.
    NANCY WILLIAMS (Lee 18 S b.Per.) Br. & --
    17 April, 1878
SMITH (see also SMYTH)
BRECKINRIDGE (Lee 20 S frm b.KY) par. -- & VA
    EUNICE D. JOHNS (Lee 17 S b.VA) par.VA & VA
    [listed as "Unice Malissa Jones" in Lee Mg]
    8 April, 1875, Lee
JOHN N. (Lee 24 S frm b.KY) par. b. KY & KY
    MARGRET SNOWDEN (Lee 20 S b.KY) par.KY & KY
    [d/o James Snowden & Lucy Thomas - BOws.]
    28 Dec., 1876, Lee
SMYTH (see also SMITH)
JOHN M. (Lee 29 2nd frm b.VA) par. b. VA & --
    LUCY E. WILLIAMS (Lee 18 S b.KY) VA & KY
    27 Nov., 1875, Lee
SNOWDEN
JOHN M. (Lee 25 S mcht. b.KY) par. b. KY & KY
    LYDIA A. THOMPSON (Lee 15 S b.KY) VA & VA
    25 March, 1875, Lee
SPICER
GRANDVILLE (Lee 18 S frm b.KY) par. b. KY & KY
    SARAH ANN ESTES (Lee 18 S b.KY) par.KY & KY
    [poss. d/o Fielding Estes - RFR]
    13 Sept., 1877, Lee
STAMPER
PETER (Lee 21 S frm b.KY) par. b. KY & KY
    [s/o Lewis Stamper & Jane Mays]
    MARY A[NN] TURNER (Lee 17 S b.KY) KY & KY
    23 June, 1876, Lee
STRONG
JAMES (Est. 23? S frm b.KY) par. b. -- & KY
    ELISABETH TOWNSEND (Lee 22 S b.KY) KY & KY
    13 Feb., 1876, Lee

THOMAS
GEORGE (Lee 22 S frm b.KY) par. b. KY & TN)
    [s/o Joseph Thomas & Eliz. Brewer - BOws.]
    SUSAN ARNOLD (Lee 20 S b.TN) par. VA & VA
    10 Sept., 1876, Lee
JAMES M. (Lee 30 S miller b.KY) par. KY & KY
    [s/o Anthony Thomas & Paulina Snowden]
    ELEAN[OR] CATH. THOMPSON (Lee 17 S b.KY)
    par. b. VA & VA
    [d/o Wm. & Polly Thompson - per deaths]
    25 March, 1875, Lee

THOMPSON
SYLVANUS (Lee 37 S frm b.Lee, VA) par. b. Lee,
    VA & VA
    SARAH ARNOLD (Lee 24 S b.VA) par. VA & VA
    - Oct, 1878, Lee [listed 24 Oct, Lee Mgs.]
TOWNSEND
GEORGE (Lee 24 S frm b.KY) par. b. KY & KY
    SENA [DULCENA] PROFITT (Lee 22 S b.KY) par.
    b. KY & KY
    9 March, 1876, Lee
TREADWAY
WM. M. (Lee 20 S frm b.Ows.)
    s/o T[homas] J & Demia Treadway [nee Lutes]
    MARY F[RANCES] BRISCOE (Lee 23 S b.Hanc,TN)
    d/o Wm. & Kitty Briscoe
    23 Aug., 1874, Lee
TURNER
DAVID (Lee 23 S frm b.Br.) par. b. Per. & Clay
    NANCY STAMPER (Lee 20 S b.Br) par. Br. & Br
    [d/o Albert Stamper & Sarah Mays]
    20 June, 1878

VANDERPOOL
JACOB W. (Lee 25 S frm b. KY) par. b. VA & KY
    VINNIA ANGEL (Lee 18 S b.KY) par. KY & KY
    [d/o Wilburn Angel & Marinda Mays]
    19 April, 1877, Lee

WARNER
WILLIAM (Est. 23 S frm b.KY) par. b. KY & KY
    MINNIA DURBIN (Lee 22 S b.KY) par. KY & KY
    13 July, 1875, Lee
WELLS
ISRAEL (Nicholas 24 S frm b.VA) par. VA & TN
    FANNIE TOWNSEND (Lee 19 S b.KY) KY & KY
    14 Dec., 1876, Lee
WILLIAM (Nicholas 24 S frm b.VA) par. -- & TN
    LUCINDA PROFITT (Lee 21 S b.KY) par.KY & KY
    7 Dec., 1876, Lee
WILLIAMS
JOHN W. F. (Lee 26 S frm b.KY) par. b. VA & KY
    ALICE C. SHEARER (Lee 18 S b.KY) par. b.
    KY & VA
    30 Dec., 1875, Lee

WILSON
DAVID (Ows. 24 S frm b.KY) par. b. KY & KY
    MARY J. GABBARD (Lee 18 S b.KY) KY & KY
    [d/o Claiborn Gabbard & Minerva Cottongim -
    RMT]
    2 Aug., 1877, Lee
WYATT
GEO. B. (Lee 21 S frm b.KY) par. b. KY & KY
    MARY TURLEY (Lee 21 S b.KY) par. b. ----
    [d/o Michael Turley & Rebecca Smith - BOws]
    24 May, 1877, Lee
WILLIAM (Lee 23 S frm b.Est.) par. Est. & Est.
    LEVIS[A] J. DUKE (Lee 16 S b.Est.) TN & Est
    6 Aug., 1878

YOUNG
HENRY (Mad. 27 S frm b.KY) par. b. VA & KY
    DELILA PALMER (Lee 18 S b.KY) par. KY & KY
    1 March, 1876, Lee
    [a/L as md. March, 1877, Henry of Lee, age
    22, rest of data same; listed Lee Co. Mgs.
    as 1 March, 1877]

BIRTH RECORDS - 1902-1904

NOTE: The top few lines of most of these
pages are blackened and unreadable.

ABNER
R[obert] T., - Jan., 1903 (M W alive Lee)
    s/o Lewis Abner & "Chester" Cockerham
    par. b. Lee & Lee; R.Lee
ARNOLD
Darsie, 11 May, 1904 (M W alive Lee)
    s/o L. D. Arnold & Georgie Lutes [see mgs]
    par. b. Lee & Lee; R.Lee
ASHCRAFT
Damen(?), 26 Oct., 1903 (M W alive Lee)
    s/o Brutis Ashcraft & Marth[a] Sparks
    par. b. Est. & Harl(?); R.Lee

BARKER
Cornealus, 27 April, 1903 (M W alive Lee)
    s/o Josep[h] Barker & Sarah Dugger
    par. b. Wlf. & Lee; R.Lee
BARRETT
James F., 11 ----?, 1902 (M W alive Lee)
    s/o John Barrett & -----? Mayse
    par. b. Lee & Lee; R.Lee
Joseph, 30 Oct., 1904 (M W alive Lee)
    s/o J[ohn] B. Barrett & Fannie Bowman
    par. b. Est. & Ows.; R.Lee
    [twin of Jossie]
Jossie, 30 Oct., 1904 (F W alive Lee)
    d/o J[ohn] B. Barrett & Fannie Bowman
    par. b. Est. & Ows.; R.Lee
    [twin of Joseph]

65

BEGLEY
Walter, 13 May, 1903 (M W alive Lee)
    s/o Hiram Begley & Sinda Evans
    par. b. Lee & Lee; R.Lee
BOOTHE
John W., 30 May, 1903 (M W alive Lee)
    s/o Geo. W. Boothe & Laura Jane Goodwin
    par. b. Wlf. & Wlf.; R.Lee
    [a/L same date 1904]
BOWMAN
Fenton, 18 April, 1903 (M W alive Lee)
    s/o Matt Bowman & Callie Coomer
    par. b. Lee & Lee; R.Lee
Samuel, 2 Feb., 1903 (M W alive Lee)
    s/o W. H. Bowman & Sarah Gabbard
    par. b. Lee & Lee; R.Lee
BRANDENBURG
Burtie, 15 July, 1903 (F W alive Lee)
    d/o John Brandenburg & Louisa Pendergrass
    par. b. Lee & Lee; R.Lee
C. C., 4 ---?, 1903 (M W alive Lee)
    s/o Lewis Brandenburg & Maryania Gilbert
    par. b. Lee & Per.; R.Lee
Efford, 19 Sept., 1903 (M W alive Lee)
    s/o Isham Brandenburg & Malvry Creech
    par. b. Ows. & Ows.; R.Ows.
Ezra, 18 Jan., 1903 (M W alive Lee)
    s/o Mat Brandenburg & Martha E. Gabbard
    par. b. Lee & Jack.; R.Lee
Marie, 2 July, 1903 (F W alive Lee)
    d/o Jas. H. Brandenburg & Martha Mays
    par. b. Lee & Lee; R.Lee
Mattie, 25 July, 1903 (F W alive Lee)
    d/o Asa Brandenburg & Alice Cole
    par. b. Lee & Lee; R.Lee
Nannie, - July, 1903 (F W alive Lee)
    d/o Simmie Brandenburg & Emeline Moore
    par. b. Lee & Ows.; R.Lee
BURK
Emmie(?), 5 ---?, 1905 (F W alive Lee)
    d/o John W. Burk & Nannie Marcum
    par. b. Lee & Ows.; R.Lee
BUTLER
Edgar, 10 July, 1903 (M W alive Lee)
    s/o Jackson Butler & Nancy Whisman
    par. b. Lee & Lee; R.Lee
    [a/L same date 1904; par. b. Per. & VA]

CABLE
Carlton, 8 Dec., 1902 ("F" W alive Lee)
    s/o Casper Cable & Frances Kincaid
    par. b. Lee & Lee; R.Lee   [see deaths]
CHILDERS
Lloyd, 15 May, 1903 (M W alive Lee)
    s/o Chas. Childers & Lucinda Spencer
    par. b. Wlf. & Lee; R.Lee
COLE
John O., 8 July, 1903 (M W alive Lee)
    s/o Medly Cole & Minnie Couch
    par. b. Lee & Lee; R.Lee
    [a/L same date 1904; mother "Fannie" Couch;
    par. b. Lee & Morg.]
COMBS
Otto, 22 Oct., 1904 (M W alive Lee)
    s/o Wm. Combs & Sarah C. Combs
    par. b. Ows. & Ows.; R.Lee
COUCH
Daisy, 14 Jan., 1903 (F W alive Lee)
    d/o Farmer Couch & Patience Johnson
    par. b. Clay & Pow.; R.Lee
    [a/L same date 1904; mom Patient "Jameson"]
Mary L., 22 ----, 1903 (F W alive)
    d/o Wm. "Crouch" & Martha Camack
    par. b. Est. & Ows.; R.Lee
    [Mary age 6 in 1910 census]
CRABTREE
Manerva, 28 March, 1903 (F W alive Lee)
    d/o James Crabtree & Ida Combs
    par. b. Lee & Lee; R.Lee
CREECH
Earl, 11 April, 1903 ("F" W alive Lee)
    s/o Floyd Creech & Lula Stamper
    par. b. Wlf. & Lee; R.Lee
Myrtle, 9 July, 1903 (F W alive Lee)
    d/o J. D. Creech & Lou E. Asbery
    par. b. Wise Co., VA & Wlf.; R.Lee
CROOK
Enos H., 28 July, 1904 (M W alive Lee)
    s/o Chas. Crook & Maud Salyers
    par. b. Lee & Wise Co., VA; R.Lee
Logan S., 27 Oct., 1902 (M W alive Lee)
    s/o C[harles] W. Crook & Maud Salyer
    par. b. Lee & Wise Co., VA; R.Ows.
    [see deaths]

CURRY
Hargnes J., 31 Aug., 1903 (M W alive Lee)
   s/o John A. Curry & Amanda Stamper
   par. b. Lee & Br.; R.Lee [see deaths]

DENNIS
C--? C--?, 28 -----?, 1903 (M? W alive Lee)
   ch/o J. P. Dennis & Sarah Curry
   par. b. Lee & Lee; R.Lee
DURBIN
---lie(?), -----? 1902/3(?) (F W alive Lee)
   d/o Walter(?) Durbin & -----? Mayse
   par. b. Lee & Lee; R.Lee

EAGER(?)
Wm. Thomas, 27 July, 1903 (M W alive Lee)
   s/o P. T. Eager(?) & -----? ----hirts(?)
   par. b. Ows. & Ows.; R.Lee
EVANS
Nannie, 15 Sept., 1903 (F W alive Lee)
   d/o Clay Evans & Lucy Damerel
   par. b. Lee & Lee; R.Lee

FARMER
Dewey, - Feb., 1903 (M W alive Lee)
   s/o John C. Farmer & Perdillia Lynch
   par. b. Lee & Est.; R.Lee
FIKE
Fred, 23 March, 1903 (M W alive Lee)
   s/o Elihue Fike & Mary J. Barrett
   par. b. Lee & Lee; R. Lee
FLANERY
Pearl, 16 Oct(?), 1902 (F W alive Lee)
   d/o Jas. Flanery & Nannie Richardson
   par. b. Lee & Lee; R.Lee

GODFREY
Nancy, 15 Sept., 1903 (F Blk alive Lee)
   d/o John Godfrey & Oma Gipson
   par. b. Br. & Lee; R.Lee
GOE
Robert B., 15 ----?, 1903 (M W alive Lee)
   s/o W. B. Goe & Willie Read
   par. b. Lee & Lee; R.Lee

GRAY
Hulbert, 22 Jan., 1903 (M W alive Lee)
    s/o H. K. Gray & Nestie B. Mays
    par. b. Lee & Lee; R.Lee

HALL
---- [Carlos P], - July, 1903 (M W alive Lee)
    s/o Charlie Hall & "Mannie" Arnold
    par. b. Lee & Lee; R.Lee [Ows. 1910 census]
Fannie, -? May(?), 1903 (F W alive Lee)
    d/o Wm. Hall & ----? Herendon
    par. b. Lee & Ows.; R.Lee
HAMILTON
---- [Elmer], 28 July, 1903 (M Blk alive Lee)
    s/o Chas. Hamilton & Mollie King
    par. b. Lee & Lee; R. Lee
---- [Willard], 11 July, 1903 (M Blk al. Lee)
    s/o Wm. Hamilton & Liza McGloson
    par. b. Lee & Lee; R.Lee
HOLLAND
Edward, 2 Feb., 1903 (M W alive Lee)
    s/o Flem Holland & Ellen Tharp
    par. b. Lee & Lee; R.Lee
HOWELL
John, 27 ----?, 1903 (M W alive Lee)
    s/o Thomas Howell & Rosie Cole
    par. b. Lee & Lee; R. Lee
HUGHS
Chas. H., b. 25 May, 1904 (M W alive Lee)
    s/o Sid Hughs & Mattie E. Howell
    par. b. Est. & Ows.; R.Lee

INGRAM
Nettie, "31" April, 1903 (F W alive Lee)
    d/o F. M. Ingram & Flora Cornett
    par. b. Est. & Lee; R.Lee

JOHNSON
-----, - March, 1903 (F W alive Lee)
    d/o Henry Johnson & Lora Williams
    par. b. Lee & Wlf.; R.Lee
Jossie, 14 Nov., 1902 (F W alive Lee)
    d/o Anderson Johnson & Dora Gabbard
    par. b. Lee & Lee; R.Lee
    [a/L same date 1904; d/o "Delina" Gabbard;
    par. b. Br. & Br.; Josie age 7 in 1910;
    Anderson & Deloria md. 1883 - RMT]

KINCAID
-----? [Carrie], -? March(?), 1903(?) (F W
    alive Lee)
    d/o R[utherford] B. Kincaid & ---? [Martha]
    par. b. Lee & Lee(?); R.Lee
Hettie, b. 18 Aug., 1903 (F W alive Lee)
    d/o Walter Kincaid & Margret J. Ingram
    par. b. Lee & Lee; R.Lee

LUCAS
E. E., 10 Feb., 1903 (M W alive Lee)
    s/o F. J. Lucas & Lillie M. Parsons
    par. b. Lee & Lee Co., VA; R.Lee
LUTES
-----, 14 March, 1903 (M W alive Lee)
    s/o F. M. Lutes & Nancy E. Kincaid
    par. b. Lee & Lee; R.Lee
Annie, 7 Aug., 1903 (F W alive Lee)
    d/o Simpson Lutes & Annie Brandenburg
    par. b. Lee & Ows.; R.Lee
---- [Fairlee], - March, 1903 (F W alive Lee)
    d/o Arch Lutes & Laura Bartlette
    par. b. Lee & ---; R.Lee
Frances, 3 Sept., 1903 (F W alive Lee)
    d/o C. C. Lutes & Annie Davis
    par. b. Lee & Lee; R.Lee
Mamy(?), 3 Oct., 1904 (F W alive Lee)
    d/o J. N. Lutes & Amanda Hall
    par. b. Lee & Lee; R.Lee
LYNCH
Wm., 21 May, 1903 (M W alive Lee)
    s/o M. E. Lynch & Mary Ann Goosey
    par. b. Ows. & Lee; R.Lee

McINTOSH
Chester, - March, 1903 (M W alive Lee)
    s/o Larkin McIntosh & Eveline Brandenburg
    par. b. Br. & Lee; R.Lee
McKENEY
Lucy, - ----?, 1903 (F W alive Lee)
    d/o Dillard(?) McKeney & Ellie(?) Tipton
    par. b. Lee & Est.; R.Lee

MARTIN
Fannie, 14 Aug., 1903 (F W alive Lee)
    d/o John W. Martin & Kate Sparks
    par. b. Lee & Lee; R.Lee

MOORE
Roxey, 6 Oct., 1903 (F W alive Lee)
   d/o W. J. Moore & Tandy Lucas
   par. b. Jack. & Lee; R.Lee
   [a/L same date 1904]

NAPIER
James M., 24 Aug., 1903 (M W alive Lee)
   s/o P. C. Napier & Mary M. Hayse
   par. b. Lee & Montg.; R.Lee
NEWTON
Edna, 25 Feb., 1903 (F W alive Lee)
   d/o Flemmon Newton & Lousinda Mayse
   par. b. Lee & Br.; R.Lee

OLINGER
G. B., - Aug., 1903 (M W alive Lee)
   s/o H. B. Olinger & Margret Creech
   par. b. Wlf. & Lee; R.Lee

PAUL
John B., 25 Aug., 1903 (M W alive Lee)
   s/o A. H. Paul & Captolia Miller
   par. b. Laurence Co., OH & Br.; R.Wlf
PRICE/PRYSE
Mary, - July, 1903 (F W alive Lee)
   d/o Moses Price & -----? Price
   par. b. Lee & Lee; R.Lee
   [appar. twin of Mattie]
Mattie(?), - July, 1903 (F W alive Lee)
   d/o Moses Pryse & -----? Price
   par. b. Lee & Lee; R.Lee
   [appar. twin of Mary]
Stanley, 10 Jan., 1903 (M W alive Lee)
   s/o W. C. Pryse & Sallie Ann Johnson
   par. b. Lee & Lee; R.Lee

RILEY
Mertie, - June, 1903 (F W alive Lee)
   d/o R. B. Riley & May Houston
   par. b. Br. & Laurel; R.Lee
ROSS
Cassie L., 12 March, 1903 (F W alive Lee)
   d/o George Ross & Nettie Webb
   par. b. Ows. & Lee; R.Lee

ROSS (cont.)
Robert, 28 Dec., 1902 (M W alive Lee)
    s/o Grant Ross & Martha Burns
    par. b. Ows. & Lee; R.Lee

SHACKELFORD
Elsie, 21 Dec., 1903 (F W alive Lee)
    d/o S. B. Shackelford & Sarah B. Stamper
    par. b. Lee & Lee; R.Lee
SHOEMAKER
Cordie, 3 March, 1903 (M W alive Lee)
    s/o Henry Shoemaker & Evaline Hayse
    par. b. Lee & Wlf.; R. Lee
Luther, 9 Dec., 1902 (M W alive Lee)
    s/o Thomas Shoemaker & Mertie Wilson
    par. b. Lee & Lee; R.Lee
SMITH
-----, 23 May, 1903 (M W alive Lee)
    s/o L. E. Smith & Janie B. Marshall
    par. b. Lee & Lee; R.Lee
Benjamin, 19 May, 1903 (M W alive Lee)
    s/o Daniel Smith & Callie Medcalf
    par. b. Lee & Lee; R.Lee
Brenis(?), 10 ----?, 1903 (F W alive Lee)
    d/o C. B. Smith & Lucy E. Cox
    par. b. Lee & Lee; R.Lee
Edna, 22 Nov., 1904 ("M" W alive Lee)
    d/o John P. Smith & Eliz. Handy
    par. b. Ows. & Ows.; R.Lee
Shirley, 14 Jan., 1903 ("M" W dead Lee)
    ch/o G. B. Smith & Sarah Stamper
    par. b. Lee & Lee; R.Lee
SPICER
-----?, -----? 1902/3(?) (F W alive Lee)
    d/o Wm. Spicer & -----? Camack
    par. b. Br. & ---?; R.Lee
STAMPER
-----, - March, 1903 (F W alive Lee)
    d/o E. J. Stamper & Catherine Amberga
    par. b. Lee & Est.; R.Lee
    [appar. twin of Minetree]
Minetree, - March, 1903 (M W alive Lee)
    s/o E. J. Stamper & Catherine Amberga
    par. b. Lee & Est.; R.Lee
    [appar. twin of unnamed female above]

STAMPER (cont.)
Pearl, - March, 1903 (F W alive Lee)
   d/o "Flored" Stamper & Sarah A. Ashcraft
   par. b. Lee & Lee; R.Lee
STEEL
Carlee Bayde, b. 5 Feb., 1903 (M W alive Lee)
   s/o Stonewall Steel & Emma Evans
   par. b. Lee & Ows.; R.Lee
Elmer, 5 June, 1903 (M W alive Lee)
   s/o Thos. Steel & Flawrence Davis
   par. b. Lee & Lee; R.Lee
STONE
Bettie, 27 April, 1903 (F W alive Lee)
   d/o Rollen Stone & Rosa Rose
   par. b. Wlf. & Lee; R.Lee
STRONG
Lillie L., 7 July, 1903 (F W alive Lee)
   d/o Andy Strong & Maggie Centers
   par. b. Lee & Lee; R.Lee
Sarah L., 28 July, 1903 (F W alive Lee)
   d/o Elija[h] Strong & Rosa B. Childers
   par. b. Lee & Lee; R.Lee
SULLIVAN
Golden, 25 Nov., 1902 (F W alive Lee)
   d/o Thos. Sullivan & Sarah Chapman
   par. b. Lee & Lee; R.Lee
   [a/L same date 1904]

THOMAS
A. F., 21 Feb., 1903 (M W alive Lee)
   s/o W. G. Thomas & Leona Napier
   par. b. Wlf. & Wlf; R.Wlf
Aron, 14 March, 1903 (M W alive Lee)
   s/o Wm. Thomas & Lizzie Thomas
   par. b. Lee & Lee; R.Lee
---- [Price], 3 April, 1903 (M W alive Lee)
   s/o M[illard] F. Thomas & Cora E.
   Comealison
   par. b. Lee & Lee; R.Lee
TOLER
Ollie, 24 Aug., 1903 (F W alive Lee)
   d/o Joseph Toler & Lyda A. Mann
   par. b. Lee & Lee; R.Lee
Willis, 26 Jan., 1903 (M W alive Lee)
   s/o J. W. Toler & Rose Couch
   par. b. Lee & Lee; R.Lee

TURNER
-----? Lee, 25 ---?, 1902 (M W alive Lee)
   s/o Cager Turner & Nancy L. "Crouch"
   par. b. Br. & Est.; R.Lee
Hellen, 30 March, 1903 (F W alive Lee)
   d/o D. G. Turner & Mollie Short
   par. b. Lee & Jack.; R.Lee

WHITE
Harland, 6 June, 1903 (M W alive Lee)
   s/o P. D. White & Netie(?) Goe
   par. b. Est. & Lee; R.Lee
WILLIAMS
Ethel M., 8 May, 1903 (F W alive Lee)
   d/o Clark Williams & Flora Shoemaker
   par. b. Lee & Lee; R.Lee
WILLSON
Berlie, 1 Sept., 1903 (F W alive Lee)
   d/o David Willson & Mary J. Gabbard
   par. b. Lee & Lee; R.Lee
   [possibly s/b Albert "Bertie" s/o David &
   Mary - RMT]

NOTE: The top few lines of one page are blackened and unreadable.

ARNOLD
G. W. (M W md; 52; frm) d. 13 Nov., 1900 of
    fever; b.TN; R.Lee; d.Lee
    s/o L. D. & Mary Arnold, b. VA & VA
L. D. (M W md; 76; frm) d. 4 Dec., 1902 of
    fever; b.Lee; R.Lee; d.Lee
    s/o Rutherford & Mary Arnold, b. ---
ASHCRAFT
Dillard [Gideon] (M W md; 64; frm) d. 30 Nov.,
    1903 of brain trouble; b.Ows.; R.Lee; d.Lee
    s/o Gillard [Gideon] & Nancy Ashcraft [nee
    Barker], b. ----

BAILEY
Jennie(?) (F W "md"; --) d. 23 March, 1901 of
    ----; b.Est.; R.Lee; d.Lee
    d/o Richard & Mary "Baley", b. Est. & Est.
BARRETT
Harges (M W S; --) d. 4 June, 1901 of -----;
    b.Lee; R.Lee; d.Lee
    s/o John & Fannie Barrett, b. Ows. & Ows.
Mattison (M W S; 3) d. 20 Dec., 1900 of croup;
    b.Lee; R.Lee; d.Lee
    s/o John & Rachel Barrett, b. Br. & Ows.
BEGLEY
Allen (M W S; 22; frm) d. 2 Sept., 1903 of
    appendicitis; b.Lee; R.Lee; d.Lee
    s/o Bradley & Sis Begley, b. Ows. & Ows.

BRANDENBURGH

Alice (- W -; --) d. 31 March, 1903 of ----;
    b.Lee; R.Lee; d.Lee
    d/o David & Louisa Brandenburg, b. Ows & Br
Carrie (F W S; 1) d. 21 Nov., 1903 of croup;
    b.Lee; R.Lee; d.Lee
    d/o Logan & Nancy Brandenburg, b. Lee & Lee
Sarah C. (F W "md"; 18; frm) d. 19 Nov., 1900
    of ---; b.Lee; R.Lee; d.Lee
    d/o D. & N. Brandenburgh, b. Lee & Lee
T. (F W md; 35) d. 23 June, 1904 of
    consumption; b.Jack.; R.Lee; d.Lee
    d/o Wm. H. & Mary COLE, b. Jack. & Wise Co,
    VA

CABLE

Carlton (M W S; 7 mo.) d. 14 July, 1903 of ---
    b.Lee; R.Lee; d.Lee
    s/o Casper & Frances Cable [nee Kincaid],
    b. Lee & Lee
Frances (F W md; 20) d. 10 Dec., 1902 of -----
    [appar d in childbirth] b.Lee; R.Lee; d.Lee
    d/o Socratis & Ann KINCAID, b. Est. & Montg
CO------?
Mary J. (F W md; 46) d. 29 Dec., 1902 of ----?
    b.--?; R.Lee; d.Lee
    d/o -----? & Sookey NEWMAN, b. -----?

CORNETT

Amanda (F W md; 28) d. 12 May, 1904 of
    consumption; b.Lee; R.Lee; d.Lee
    d/o Henry & Delina ROSS, b. Ows. & Ows.
Eva (F W S; 17) d. 28 April, 1904 of
    consumption; b.Lee; R.Lee; d.Lee
    d/o P. C. & Mary Cornett, b. Lee & Ows.
Martha (F W S; 1) d. 28 Sept., 1904 of
    consumption; b.Lee; R.Lee; d.Lee
    d/o Brand & Amanda Cornett, b. Lee & Lee

COUCH

Margaret A. (F W md; 45) d. 28 April, 1904 of
    consumption; b.Lee; R.Lee; d.Lee
    d/o Kaner & Jane SMITH, b. Lee & Lee

CRABTREE

Ida (F W md; 22) d. 16 Aug., 1903 of
    bronchitis; b.Lee; R.Lee; d.Lee
    d/o Ned & Armina COMBS, b. ----

CREECH

Martha (F W md; 65) d. 11 May, 1903 of
consumption; b.NC; R.Lee; d.Lee
d/o Tho. & Elizabeth PATERSON, b. ----

Martha (F W md; 18) d. 26 April, 1904 of ----;
b.Lee; R.Lee; d.Lee
d/o Grant & Armina DEATON, b. Per. & Br.

CROOK

Logan S. (M W S; 2) d. 18 Sept, 1904 of
Membranus croup; b.Lee; R.Lee; d.Lee
s/o Chas. & Maud Crook [nee Salyer], b. Lee
& Wise Co, VA

CURRY

Amandy (F W md; 30) d. 1 Dec., 1903 of
consumption; b.Lee; R.Lee; d.Lee
d/o Edward & Tilda STAMPER [nee Turner], b.
Br. & Br.

Charles W. (M W S; 22; frm) d. 2 July, 1904 of
fever; b.Lee; R.Lee; d.Lee
s/o James & Luviny(?) Curry, b. Lee & Lee

Hargis (M W S; 1) d. 3 Aug., 1904 of flux;
b.Lee; R.Lee; d.Est.
s/o John & Amanda Curry [nee Stamper], b.
Lee & Lee   [see Amanda's death above]

James M. (M W md; 57; frm) d. 18 July, 1903 of
consumption; b.Lee; R.Lee; d.Lee
s/o Wm. & Ellen Curry, b. ----

DUNAGIN

Clara (F W S; 16) d. 20 Feb., 1901 of ----;
b.Lee; R.Lee; d.Lee
d/o L. & F. Dunagin, b. Lee & Lee

Edna (F W S; 4) d. 10 April, 1901 of ----;
b.Lee; R.Lee; d.Lee
d/o L. & F. Dunagin, b.-----

DUNAWAY

Clide (M W S; 1) d. 18 Dec., 1900 of -----;
b.Lee; R.Lee; d.Lee
s/o John & Sarah Dunaway, b. Lee & Lee

EDITINGTON (ELINGTON?)

Bean (M W S; 2) d. 9 Sept., 1903 of croup;
b.Lee; R.Lee; d.Lee
s/o Ed & Eliza "Elington", b. Greenup & Lee

EVANS

Jesse (M W md; 70; frm) d. 8 Sept., 1903 of
; b.Ows.; R.Lee; d.Lee
s/o Jesse & Edaom Evans, b. Ows. & --

FIKE

Stanley (M W S; 11) d. 25 July, 1901, drowned;
b.Lee; R.Lee; d.Lee
s/o Elihue & Mary Fike [nee Barrett], b.
Ows. & Ows.

FOX

Thomas (M W md.; 50; frm) d. 13 Dec., 1900 of
; b.Br.; R.Lee; d.Lee
s/o John & Sally Fox, b. TN & TN

GILBERT

Herbert (M W S; 8; frm) d. 18 June, 1903 of
flux; b.Lee; R.Lee; d.Lee
s/o Thomas & Mary A. Gilbert, b. Ows. & Ows
John H. (M W S; 18; frm) d. 18 June, 1903 of
flux; b.Lee; R.Lee; d.Lee
s/o Thomas & Mary A. Gilbert, b. Ows. & Ows

GREER (GREEN?)

I. J. (F W S; 1) d. 6 April, 1901 of brain
fever; b.Lee; R.Lee; d.Lee
d/o Jesse & Frances "Green", b. Lee & Lee

GROSS

William N. (M W S; 1) d. 6 June, 1904 of flux;
b.Lee; R.Lee; d.Lee
s/o Ned & Julia A. Gross, b. Br. & Br.

HALL

Harvey (M W md; 50; frm) d. - April, 1901 of
fever; b.Ows.; R.Lee; d.Lee
s/o Henry & Mary Hall, b. ---
Leslie (M W S; 17; frm) d. 14 Oct., 1900,
"kild" by saw; b.Lee; R.Lee; d.Lee
s/o H. H. & Callie Hall, b. Lee & Lee

HAMMAN

Thomas M. (M W S; 14) d. - Jan., 1903 of
fever; b.Lee; R.Lee; d.Lee
s/o B. F. & Sindar Hamman, b. ----

HORN(?)

y(?) (M W md; ---?) d. - June, 1903(?)
of ?; b.--?; R.--?; d.--?
s/o ?

JOHNSON
Lilly M. (F W S; 23) d. - April, 1903 of ----;
    b.Lee; R.Lee; d.Lee
    d/o James & Nannie Johnson, b. Lee & Ows.
Wm. (M W S; 1) d. 27 May, 1903 of flux;
    b.Lee; R.Lee; d.Lee
    s/o S. & Sopha Johnson, b. Pow. & Ows.
JONES
Orca (F W S; --) d. 12 April, 1901 of -----;
    b.Lee; R.Lee; d.Lee
    d/o Henry & Mollie Jones, b. Lee & Lee
Otta (F W S; --) d. 13 April, 1901 of ------;
    b.Lee; R.Lee; d.Lee
    d/o Henry & Mollie Jones, b. Lee & Lee

KELLEY
-----? (M W md; -5?; frm) d. 31 July, 1903
    of consumption; b.Ows?; R.Lee; d.Lee
    s/o -----------?
KEYWOOD
Axie (F Blk S; 6) d. 15 Aug., 1901 of fever;
    b.Lee; R.Lee; d.Lee
    d/o Henry & Mary Keywood, b. Harl. & John.

LUTES
Dudley P. (M W S; 17) 9 Dec., 1902 of flux
    b.Lee; R.Lee; d.Lee
    s/o F. M. & Evoline Lutes, b. Lee & Lee

McGUIRE
A[rchibald] C. ("F" W S; 22) d. 6 Nov., 1903
    of consumption; b.Lee; R.Lee; d.Lee
    s/o Thomas & Margret McGuire [nee Thomas],
    b. Est. & Ows.
McINTOSH
Lennie (F W S; 4) d. - June, 1903 of flux;
    b.Lee; R.Lee; d.Lee
    d/o ------? & Melviny(?) McIntosh, b. Br.
    & Ows.
Robert (M W S; 12) d. - June, 1903 of flux;
    b.Lee; R.Lee; d.Lee
    s/o ------? & Melviny(?) McIntosh, b. Br.
    & Ows.
McKENEY
-----? (F W md; --?) d. 12(?) Aug., 1903 of
    consumption; b.--?; R.Lee(?); d.Lee
    d/o -----? & Marget KELLY; b. -----?

MARSHALL
Alfred (M W S; --) d. - April, 1903 of ----;
    b.Lee; R.Lee; d.Lee
    s/o ----------

NEWMAN
John (M W md; 37; frm) d. 5 March, 1901 of
    consumption; b.Lee; R.Lee; d.Lee
    s/o John & E. Newman, b. Ows. & Ows.
NEWTON
John (M W md; 36/56? frm) d. 30 July, 1901 of
    -----; b.Est.; R.Lee; d.Lee
    s/o Allen & Rachel Newton, b. Est. & Est.
Nancy (F W S; 4) d. - April, 1903 of -----;
    b.Est.; R.Lee; d.Lee
    d/o Flemmon & Lucinda Newton [nee Mays], b.
    Lee & Lee

PALMER/PARMER
Jerry (M W S; 18; frm) d. 10 Aug., 1904 of
    nervous dis[order]; b.Lee; R.Lee; d.Lee
    s/o Link & Mary Parmer, b. Per. & Br.
Link (M W md.; 39; frm) d. 14 July, 1901 of
    consumption; b.Lee; R.Lee; d.Lee
    s/o Rubin & Marion Palmer, b. Ows. & Ows.
PRYSE
Louellen(?) ("M" W -; 20?) d. - April, 1904 of
    appendicitis; b.Lee; R.Lee; d.Lex.
    d/o Thos. & S. E. Pryse, b. Wales & Ows.

RASNER
Wm. (M W S; 28; frm) d. 22 Aug., 1901 of
    consumption; b.Ows.; R.Lee; d.Lee
    s/o Noah & Polly Rasner, b.----
ROACH
Amanda (F W -; --) d. 23 Nov., 1900, burnt;
    b.Lee; R.Lee; d.Lee
    d/o Felix & Annie COLE, b. Lee & Lee
Liddia M. (F W S; 1) d. - July, 1901 of flux;
    b.Lee; R.Lee; d.Lee
    d/o Thomas & R. Roach, b. Lee & Lee
ROLLEN
Ida (F W md; 26) d. 14 Sept, 1903 of
    consumption; b.Lee; R.Lee; d.Lee
    d/o Wm. & Pollyann COMEALISON, b. Ows & Ows

SAMPLES (STAMPER?)
Jesse (M W md; 26; frm) d. 10 May, 1903 of
   gun shot wound; b.Est.; R.Lee; d.Lee
   s/o Jackson & Nancy "Stamper", b. VA &
   Russell Co., VA
SAMS
Wm. H. (M W S; 1) d. 19 Nov., 1900 of fever;
   b.Lee; R.Lee; d.Lee
   s/o Helm(?) & Emily Sams, b. Lee & Lee
SEALE
Leah (F W md; -8?) d. 18 May, 1903 of
   consumption; b.Ows; R.Lee; d.Lee
   d/o Buch & Rane COUCH, b. -- & Lee
SMALLWOOD
Martha (F W S; 3) d. 28 Dec., 1900 of
   Diptheria; b.Lee; R.Lee; d.Lee
   d/o John & Annie Smallwood, b. Lee & Lee
SMYTH
Lou (F W md; -7?) d. 24 March, 1901 of -----;
   b.Lee; R.Lee; d.Lee
   d/o L. K. & L. CRABTREE, b. Est. & Est.
Routh(?) (F W "md"; --) d. 23 June, 1901 of
   -----; b.Lee; R.Lee; d.Lee
   d/o Wm. & Lou Smyth, b. Est. & Est.
SNOWDEN
Russel (M W S; 6) d. 26 Aug., 1901 of
   Diptheria; b.Lee; R.Lee; d.Lee
   s/o Letcher & Laura Snowden, b. Lee & Lee
SPICER
Ellis (F W wd; 65) d. 27 Feb., 1904 of dropsy;
   b.Br.; R.Lee; d.Lee
   d/o Lewis & Millie STAMPER [nee Turner], b.
   Per. & Br. [wf/o Samuel Spicer]
STAMPER
(see SAMPLES)
STEELE
Florence (F W md; 34) d. 7 June, 1903 of
   consumption; b.Lee; R.Lee; d.Lee
   d/o Thomas & Marget McGUIRE, b. Ows. & Ows.
John (M W md; 35; frm) d. - Aug., 1904 of
   cancer; b.Ows.; R.Lee; d.Lee
   s/o --------------; b. Jack. & Wise Co., VA

TAYLOR
Albert (M W md; 27; frm) d. 27 June, 1903 of
   dropsy; b.Lee; R.Lee; d.Lee
   s/o "Jane" & Nancy Taylor, b. TN & Fletcher

THOMAS

-----? (M W S; --) d. - Sept., 1904 of flux;
   b.Lee; R.Lee; d.Lee
   s/o Wm. & Eliz. Thomas, b. Jack. & Wise Co,
   VA

Elizabeth (F W "md"; 35) d. - Sept., 1904 of
   flux; b.Lee; R.Lee; d.Lee
   d/o James & Mary "Thomas", b. Jack. & Wise
   Co., VA

S. P. (M W md; 22; frm) d. 28 Aug., 1903 of
   fever; b.Lee; R.Lee; d.Lee
   s/o Henry & Jane Thomas, b. Est. & Lee, VA

TINCHER

Asa L. (M W --; 55; ---) d. 1 March, 1903 of
   consumption; b.Ows.; R.Ows.; d.Ows.
   s/o Elisha & Martha Tincher, b. Ows. & Ows.

TURNER

Amand[a] H. (F W md; 29) d. 13 Nov., 1900 of
   ----; b.Lee; R.Lee; d.Lee
   d/o Wm. & M. COMBS, b. VA & Ows.
   [wf/o Richard Turner]

VIRES

Barthena (F W md; 19) d. 13 July, 1903 of ----
   b.Lee; R.Lee; d.Lee
   d/o Henry & Annie CLARK, b. ----

WATSON

Rebecca (F W md; 65) d. 13 April, 1901 of ----
   b.Est.; R.Lee; d.Lee
   d/o Aaron & Elihue(?) HORN(?), b.Est. & Est

MARRIAGE RECORDS
1902-1904, 1907-1908, & 1910

NOTE: The top few lines of the first page are torn, blackened, and unreadable. One of the grooms was (Lee 25 S frm) and the other groom was (Lee 19 S frm). The rest is unreadable.

----RBLE(?)
ROLLIE (21 S frm b.Ows.) par. b. ----
    MARY ISAACS (Lee 16 S b.Ows.) par. b. ----
    6 Aug., 1904, Lee

ABNER
BUCK (Lee 22 S frm b.Lee) par. b. ----
    LELER DAVIS (Lee 17 S b.Lee) par. b. ----
    6 July, 1904, Lee
LEWIS (Lee 22 S lab. b.Est.) par. b. ----
    CALLIE NEWMAN (Lee 14 S b.Lee) par. b. ----
    21 May, 1904, Lee
VERNEN (Est. 19 S frm b.Est.) par. Est. & Est.
    EFFIE SMITH (Lee 16 S b.Lee) par. Lee & Lee
    12 Aug., 1910 @ George Smith's
ABNEY
MILES (Pow. 23 S frm b.Pow.) par. b. ----
    ROXSIE J. RODGERS (Lee 16 S Est.) par. ----
    19 May, 1904, Lee
ABSHEAR
ARTHUR (Lee 23 S pub.wks. b.Ows.) Ows. & Ows.
    NANNIE ROWLAND (Lee 13 S b.Ows) Ows. & Ows.
    30 July, 1908 @ James -----?; aff. filed

AKERS
AMON B. (Lee 36 2nd mcht. b.Lee) par. b. ----
    ARMILDA HOGAN (Lee 17 S b.Lee) par. b. ----
    24 Nov., 1904, Lee
ALEXANDER
C. H. (Campton 25 - --- b.KY) par. b. KY & KY
    GEORGIE STRONG (Lee 17 S b.KY) par. KY & KY
    5 Nov., 1910, Beattyville
ALLEN
HARRIS C. (Filmore 27 S Tel.Op. b.KY) KY & Lee
    NANNIE LUCAS (Monica 21 S b.KY) KY & KY
    15 Oct., 1910 @ Jesse Lucas'
W. B. (Filmore 21 S --- b.Clay) Wlf. & Lee
    LILLIE JOHNSON (Monica 17 S b.Lee) par. b.
    Lee & Lee
    17 Aug., 1910 @ W. J. Johnson's
WM. (Banford 55 2nd frm b.Br.) par. VA & Per.
    MAGGIE DEATEN (Banford 40 2nd b.Br.) par.
    b. Per. & --
    29 Jan., 1910, Banford
ANGEL
W. J. (Lee 26 S frm b.Lee) par. b. ----
    SALLIE WATKINS (Lee 23 S b.Lee) par. b. ---
    25 Dec., 1903, Lee
ARNOLD/ARNEL
J. C. (Monica 35 3rd frm b.Lee) par. Lee & Lee
    MAGGIE NORMAN (Lee 26 S b.Br.) Lee & Br.
    16 Jan., 1910 @ Thos. Johnson's
JOHN (Heidleburg 43 2nd Lum.Insp. b.--) ----
    CATTIE PIGG (Banford 40 S b.Lee) par. b.
    VA & Jack.
    5 June, 1910, Heidleberg, KY
JOSEPH (Lee 30 2nd frm b.Lee) par. b. ----
    ALICE DUNIGAN (Lee 30 2nd Pow.) par. ----
    22 Sept., 1907, Monica, KY; affidavit filed
L. D. (Lee 26 S frm b.Lee) par. b. Lee & Lee
    GEORGIA E. LUTES (Lee 19 S b.Lee) Lee & Lee
    31 Dec., 1903, Lee
ASHCRAFT
FRANK (Lee 22 S frm b.Lee) par. Lee & Est.
    FANNY HOGAN (Lee 22 S b.Lee) par. Ows & Lee
    14 Nov, 1907 @ Jim Hogan's; affidavit filed
JOHN W. (Lee 22 S frm b.--) par. b. ----
    BERTHA POWELL (Lee 14 S b.--) par. b. ----
    19 Nov, 1903, Lee

84

BACK
WILLIAM (Br. 22 S frm b.KS) par b. Br. & Br.
    MARIAM KINCAID (Lee 22 S b.Lee) par. ----
    13 Aug., 1908 @ bride's house
BAILEY
CHARLEY (Lee 22 S frm b.Wlf) par. b. ----
    NANNIE ABNER (Lee 22 S b.Lee) par. b. ----
    18 May, 1904, Lee
EVERET S. (Frankfort 22 S steno. b.Ows.) ----
    KATE M. FLANERY (Ows. 25 S b.Ows.) par. ---
    24 Dec., 1904, Lee
G. A. (Lee 48 2nd mcht. b.Br) par. Harl. & Lee
    ZILLA SIZEMORE (Lee 34 2nd b.Ows) Ows & Ows
    14 May, 1908 @ Co. Clerk's office
BAKER
OSCAR (Lee 21 S lab. b.--) par. b. ----
    MINNIE COMBS (Lee 14 S b.--) par. b. ----
    24 Oct., 1903, Lee
WM. R. (Lee 18 S frm b.Lee) par. b. Lee & NC
    MANERVA PENDERGRASS (Lee 17 S b.Lee) par.
    b. Lee & Rockc.
    12 March, 1908 @ J. Pendergrass'; bride's
    father's affidavit
BANKS
MOSES (--- 21 S frm b.Lee) par. b. ----
    GETHA TREADWAY (Lee 16 S b.Lee) par. b. ---
    17 March, 1904, Lee
BARKER
WILLIAM (Lee 19 S frm b.--) par. b. ----
    ELLA BALL (Lee 19 S b.--) par. b. ----
    6 Jan., 1904, Lee
BARRETT
G. B. (Ows. 23 S frm b.Harl) par. Br. & Harl.
    DORA PALMER (Ows. 18 2nd b.Ows) Ows. & Ows.
    2 Oct., 1907 @ Major L. Bowman's(?); aff.
    filed
JESSE (Lee 19 S frm b.Lee) par. b. ----
    MAGGIE PALMER (Lee 15 S b.Lee) par. b. ----
    21 April, 1904, Lee
BEAN
BURELL (Beattyv. 47 3rd miner b.KY) KY & Lee
    MARY McGUIER(?) (Proctor 35 3rd b.KY) par.
    b. KY & KY
    22 Oct., 1910

BEATTY
RICHARD C (Lee 25 2nd frm b.Lee) par. Lee & Br
    MABEL LUTES (Lee 23 S b.Lee) par. Lee & Lee
    16 Aug., 1908 @ Milo Beatty Jr.'s
BEGLEY
FLOYD (Pine Grove 23 S frm b.Lee) par. KY & KY
    MARY HALL (Lee 28 S b.Lee) par. Lee & --
    27 Aug., 1910 @ J. C. Hall's
H. P. (Lee 22 S frm b.Lee) par. Leslie & Lee
    BESSIE C. COLE (Lee 19 S b.Lee) Ows. & VA
    25 Dec., 1907 @ John Cole's; aff. filed
KAMMON (Lee 18 S frm b.Per) par. -- & Per.
    ANNA BELLE ESTES (Lee 17 S b.Lee) Est & Est
    [d/o Wm. Estes & Laurinda Estes - RFR]
    12 Dec, 1907 @ Wm. Estes'; affidavit filed
BELCHER
WESLEY (Lee 22 S mining b.Ows) par. Per. & Per
    MOLLIE MONTGOMERY (Lee 34 2nd b.Boyd) par.
    b. Boyd & OH
    17 Oct., 1907 @ groom's
BENTON
JESSE (Est. 39 2nd frm b.--) par. b. ----
    SARAH HORN (Lee 24 S b.--) par. b. ----
    24 Oct., 1903, Lee
BLACKWELL
EARNEST (Lee 23 S frm b.Lee) par. b. ----
    OLLIE CURRY (Lee 20 S b.Lee) par. b. ----
    24 Dec., 1903, Lee
BOUTH
CLAUDE L. (Mercer 31 2nd Ins.Agt. b.Jeff.)
    par. b. Mercer & Fay.
    LULU MORGAN (Lee 24 S b.Clay) Clay & Clay
    5 Aug., 1908 @ bride's home
BOWLING
KENIS (Lee 21 S miner b.Pittsburg, KY) par. b.
    VA & Lee
    NANNIE SPARKS (Lee 18 S b.Lee) Lee & Lee
    20 Aug., 1908 @ bride's home; aff. filed
BOWMAN
BARNEY (Athol 19 S frm b.Lee) par. Ows. & --
    LAURA STACY (Lee 16 S b.Lee) par. Lee & Lee
    27 Jan., 1910 @ Mart Stacy's
BEDFORD (Lee 25 S frm b.Br.) par. b. Br. & VA
    JESSE [JESSIE] CREECH (Lee 20 S b.Lee) par.
    b. Lee & Br.
    12 Jan., 1910 @ bride's house

BOWMAN (cont.)
DAN (Lee 25 S pub.wks. b.Ows.) par. b. ----
    ANNIE STACY (Lee 19 S b.Ows.) par. b. ----
    10 April, 1908 @ Heidelburg; bride's
    mother's affidavit
ELISHA (Lee 30 S timberman b.Lee) Ows. & --
    JANE BARRETT (Lee 23 2nd b.--) par. b. ---
    12 April, 1908 @ S. McIntosh's; aff. filed
BRANDENBURG
ARCH (Earnestv. 17 S frm b.KY) par.b. KY & Lee
    CORA BRANDENBERG (Lee 17 S b.KY) KY & KY
    10 Nov., 1910 @ Mariah Jackson's
BROWNLOW (Lee 18 S frm b.Lee) par. Ows. & Ows.
    NANCY ANN BEGLEY (Lee 19 S b.Lee) par. b.
    Leslie & Leslie
    23 July, 1908 @ A. Begley's; aff. filed
CANT (Lee 21 S frm b.Ows.) par. b. Lee & Lee
    NETTIE STACY (Lee 19 S b.Lee) Lee & Lee
    2 Feb., 1908 @ D. Brandenburg's; aff. filed
CHAS. (Ows. 29 S frm b.Ows.) par. b. ----
    ALICE STERNBURG (Lee 21 S b.Lee) par. ----
    3 Nov., 1904, Lee
DAVID (Ows. 25 S lab. b.Ows.) par. b. ----
    CLARKIE FARMER (Lee 15 S b.Lee) par. b. ---
    13 Oct., 1904, Lee
FLOYD (Lee 21 S frm b.Lee) par. b. Lee & Lee
    OLLIE SMITH (Lee 18 S b.Lee) par. Ows & Lee
    18 April, 1908 @ bride's home; aff. filed
JAMES C. (Lee 33 S mcht. b.Lee) par. Ows. & TN
    CALLIE SMITH (Lee 19 S b.Lee) Ows. & Ows.
    12 Dec, 1907 @ Huram Smith's; aff. filed
JERRY (Lee 18 S frm b.Lee) par. b. Ows. & Ows.
    SELIA PARKER (Lee 16 S b.Lee) par. Ows & Br
    23 Dec., 1902, Lee
MORGAN (Monica 23 S frm b.Lee) par. Lee & --?
    ADDA SPENCER (Filmore 21 S b.Lee) Lee & --
    1 Sept., 1910 @ S. Spence[r]'s
R. R. (Lee 21 S. barber b.Lee) par. Ows. & TN
    CYNTHIA A. KINDRICK (Lee 16 S b.Lee) par.
    b. Ows. & Lee
    5 March, 1908 @ H. Kindrick's; bride's
    father's affidavit
ROBERT (Lee 22 S frm b.Lee) par. b. ----
    ADA BAILEY (Lee 17 S b.Lee) par. b. ----
    27 Oct., 1904, Lee

BRANDENBURG (cont.)
SHELBY (Lee 23 S frm b.Lee) par. b. ----
    LAURA NORMAN (Lee 17 S b.Lee) par. b. ----
    2 Sept., 1907 @ Alford Norman's; guardian's
    affidavit
SIMPSON (Lee 25 S frm b.KY) par. b. KY & Lee
    FLORENCE KILBURN (Lee 17 S b.KY) KY & KY
    3 Nov., 1910 @ Martin Kilburn's
T. Q(?) (Lee 29 S frm b.Lee) par. b. Ows & Lee
    LIZZIE McCLANCEY (Lee 25 S b.Lee) Lee & Lee
    21 April, 1908 @ Co. Clerk's office
THOMAS F. (Lee 27 2nd brakeman b.Ows.) par. b.
    Lee & Jack.
    LOU UNDERWOOD (Lee 16 S b.Lee) Lee & Lee
    28 Sept., 1907 @ bride's house; aff. filed
BRISK
CAIN (Lee 24 2nd frm b.--) par. b. ----
    NANNIE RANKINS (Lee 17 S b.--) par. b. ----
    14 Jan., 1904, Lee
BROWN
WILSON (St.Helens 22 S frm b.Clay) VA & Lee
    HALLIE HOGAN (St.Helens 17 S b.Lee) par. b.
    IN & Lee
    25 Aug., 1910 @ Harrison Hogan's
BRYCRAFT(?)
VAUGHN (Lee 32 2nd lab. b.--) par. b. ----
    NANNIE INGRAM (Lee 22 S b.--) par. b. ----
    25 Feb., 1904, Lee
BURK
CHAS. B. (Lee 24 S bookkeeper b.Lee) par. ----
    PROVIE HOOVER (Lee 18 S b.Est.) par. b. ---
    28 Sept., 1904, Lee
MASTON (Delrinta 19 S frm b.KY) par. KY & Lee
    ELIZ. MARCUM (Delrinta 16 S b.KY) KY & KY
    22 Dec., 1910 @ A. J. Marcum's
BURNS
BRICE (Lee 57 2nd frm b.Ows.) par. b. ----
    ADA A. SMITH (Lee 45 2nd b.Ows.) par. ----
    22 Dec., 1904, Lee
MERIDA (Idamay 19 S frm b.Lee) par. KY & KY
    LENE ANDERSON (Idamay 14 S b.KY) KY & KY
    14 Sept., 1910 @ Co. Clerk's Office
BURTON
J. J. (Lee 21 S frm b.NC) par. b. ----
    LEWELLEN EDWARDS (Lee 22 S b.Lee) par. ----
    8 June, 1904, Lee

BUTLER
DAVID (Lee 19 S frm b.Br.) par. b. Br. & Br.
    MARTHA COLE (Lumber Point 15 S b.Lee) par.
    b. Lee & North --
    28 July, 1910 @ Jas. Cole's
JOHN D. (Lee 21 S frm b.--) par. b. ----
    LILLIE TOLER (Lee 17 S b.--) par. b. ----
    2 Dec., 1903, Lee

CABLE
THOMAS A. (Lee 25 S frm b.Wlf.) par. NC & Wlf.
    LINDA S. KINCAID (Lee 19 S b.Lee) Ows & Ows
    2 July, 1908 @ bride's home; aff. filed
CALDWELL
JONAS (Est. 21 S RR b.Est.) par. b. ----
    ELLIE GREEN SMITH (Lee 16 S b.Lee) Lee & Br
    5 Oct., 1907 @ Geo. Smith's; bride's
    father's affidavit
CALMES
WM. (Br. 32 S lab. b.Br.) par. b. Br. & Br.
    KITTIE BROOKS (Jack. 30 2nd b.Pow) par. b.
    Pow. & Montg.
    2 July, 1908 @ Mint(?) Wilson's; both of
    age
CAMASK
ALBERT (--- 21 S frm b.Clay) par. b. ----
    SARAH M. SPICER (Lee 17 S b.Lee) par. ----
    17 March, 1904, Lee
CAMASK(?)
HENRY (Lee 18 S frm b.Montg.) par. b. Br. &
    Carter(?)
    EVA RILEY (Lee 14 S b.Jack) par. Br. & Jack
    28 Feb., 1908 @ Dan Riley's; aff. filed
CAMPBELL
SAM E. (Lee 31 2nd lumberman b.Per.) Per & Per
    RACHEL FRYE (Lee 21 S b.Clay) par.VA & Clay
    20 June, 1908 @ L & A Depot, Beattyville;
    certificate
CARROLL
C. C. (Est. 28 S frm b.Clay) par. Clay & Clay
    NANCY BELLE FOX (Est. 22 S b.Est) Est & Est
    5 May, 1908 @ Co. Clerk's office; aff.filed
KENETH (Idamay 25 S miner b.KY) par. KY & Lee
    MARTHA STEPHENS (Lee 25 S b.KY) par.KY & KY
    2 Dec., 1910 @ Wm. Collins'

CARSON
ROBT. (Lee 22 S frm b.Lee) par. b. ----
    LAURA WILSON (Lee 17 S b.Lee) par. b. ----
    24 Dec., 1903, Lee
CARTRIGHT
N[APOLEON] B. JR. (Lee 21 S miner b.Laurel)
    par. b. Scott, VA & Scott, VA
    MATTIE STRONG (Lee 21 S b.Br) par. Br. & Br
    [d/o Sallie per 1910 census]
    1 Oct., 1908 @ bride's home; both of age
CHAMBERS
WEEDEN (Lee 20 S frm b.Br.) par. b. ----
    ADIE FOX (Lee 18 S b.Lee) par. b. ----
    22 Dec., 1904, Lee
CHILDERS
CURT (KY 27 S millman b.Wlf) par. Wlf. & Wlf.
    BERTHA COMBS (Lee 21 S b.Br) par. Br. & Lee
    9 March, 1910 @ Henry Combs'
CLARK
JAMES C. (TN 28 S frm b.TN) par. b. ----
    WRENNA SHULL (Lee 17 S b.Est.) Mad. & Lee
    27 Jan., 1903, Lee
COLE
LOGAN (Lee 21 S miner b.Lee) par. b. Lee & Lee
    KATE HORN (Lee 16 S b.Lee) par. Est. & Ows.
    28 May, 1908 @ Aaron Horn's; aff. filed
ROBT. H. (Tallega 20 S frm b.Ows.) Ows. & Ows.
    ALICE BANNET (Tallega 16 S b.Lee) KY & KY
    21 April, 1910 @ A. J. Bannett's
STANLEY (Proctor 26 S miner b.Lee) par. TN & -
    LIZZIE CLUTCH (Idamay 20 S b.Whitley) par.
    b. Lee & --
    7 May, 1910, Proctor
COLLINS
HOWARD (St.Helens 67 2nd frm b.Br.) Br. & Br.
    MAY SUTTON (St.Helens 26 2nd Beattyvl) par.
    b. Br. & Br.
    26 July, 1910, St. Helens
COLLY
H. H. (Lee 39 2nd Tel.Op. b.--) par. b. ----
    CATHERINE McGUIRE (Lee 28 S b.--) par. ---
    19 Nov., 1903, Lee
COMBS
DILLAS (Br. 22 S lab. "colored" b.Per.) ----
    CALLIE MINTER (Lee 19 S b.Ows.) par. ----
    1 Jan., 1908 @ Bill Crawford's; bride's
    father's affidavit

COMBS (cont.)

ELBERT (Lee 23 2nd frm b.Ows.) par. -- & Ows.
    ALICE FOX (Lee 27 S b.Ows.) Par. Br. & Lee
    10 Oct, 1907 @ John Shoemaker's; aff. filed
J. G. (Leighton 27 S millman b.Ows.) Ows. & --
    ALICE METCALF (Lee 15 S b.Jack) Jack.& Jack
    20 Jan., 1910 @ bride's home
JAMES (Lee 20 S frm b.Wlf.) par. b. ----
    ARA RATLIFF (Lee 20 S b.Clay) par. b. ----
    20 Oct., 1904, Lee
JOHN (Lee 22 S teamster b.Lee) par. b. ----
    NANNIE BARRETT (Lee 24 2nd b.Lee) par. ----
    4 Aug., 1904, Lee
OSCAR (Br. 25 S frm b.Br.) par. b. Br. & Br.
    NANCY TURNER (Br. 23 S b.TN) par. -- & Br.
    3 Jan., 1908 @ Co. Clerk's office
S. L. (Lee 33 S mcht. b.Ows.) par. b. ----
    MAUD DAVIDSON (Lee 19 S b.Per.) par. b. ---
    20 June, 1904, Lee
WALTER (Lee 19 S frm b.--) par. b. ----
    MAGGIE EASTES (Lee 18 S b.--) par. b. ----
    24 Dec., 1903, Lee

CONKWRIGHT

MELVIN (Lee 21 S lab. b.Montg.) par. b. ----
    ELLEN SMITH (Lee 17 S b.Est.) par. b. ----
    10 June, 1904, Lee

COOMER

ABB (Lee 22 S frm b.--) par. b. ----
    LAURA CUNDIFF (Lee 18 S b.--) par. b. ----
    25 Dec., 1903, Lee
ANDY (Lee 25 S frm b.Lee) par. b. ----
    ELLEN ESTES (Lee 15 S b.Lee) par. b. ----
    15 Dec., 1904, Lee
LOGAN (Lee 20 S frm b.Lee) par. b. ----
    SARAH THOMAS (Lee 18 S b.VA) par. b. ----
    11 Aug., 1904, Lee
TOM (Lee 20 S miner b.Lee) par. b. ----
    ALLICE CORNETT (Lee 20 S b.Lee) par. ----
    20 Oct., 1904, Lee

COOPER

THOS. W. (Lee 24 S frm b.Lee) par. Ows. & --
    JANE JUDD (Lee 18 S b.Lee) par. Ows. & Br.
    20 Aug., 1903, Lee

COUCH

ALBERT (Lee 22 S frm b.--) par. b. ----
   AMANDA COUCH (Lee 16 S b.Ows.) par. b. ----
   15 July, 1904, Lee

ALBERT (Lee 18 S frm b.Lee) par. b. Lee & Lee
   BARTHENA PUCKETT (Lee 16 S b.Lee) Lee & Lee
   17 June, 1908 @ Jim Couch's; aff. filed

GEO. (Lee 21 S frm b.Lee) par. b. ----
   ELIS DUNAWAY (Lee 19 S b.Lee) par. ----
   13 Oct., 1904, Lee

JAMES (Lee 18 S frm b.Lee) par. b. ----
   SALLIE B. SPICER (Lee 16 S b.Br.) par. ---
   22 Nov., 1904, Lee

SIMP (Lee 25 S frm b.Ows.) par. b. ----
   SARAH FOX (Lee 16 S b.Lee) par. b. ----
   24 March, 1904, Lee

SIMP (Beattyvl 30 2nd lab. b.KY) par. KY & Lee
   METTIE SPICER (Lee 17 S b.KY) par. KY & KY
   8 Nov., 1910 @ Ned Spicer's

CRAWFORD

JERRY (Lee 29 2nd frm b.Br.) par. b. ----
   ALLISE STAMPER (Lee 23 S b.Lee) par. -----
   15 June, 1904, Lee

CREECH

ROBT. (Lee 21 S frm b.--) par. b. ----
   CATHERINE DEATON (Lee 16 S b.--) par. b. --
   23 Dec., 1903, Lee

STEPHEN (Lee 23 2nd frm b.Lee) par. b. ----
   CALLIE DEATON (Lee 18 S b.Lee) par. b. ----
   [d/o Green Deaton & Sarah Spencer]
   18 Oct., 1904, Lee

CROOK

WILLIAM (Lee 28 S lab. b.Lee) par. b. ----
   ROXSIE BURK (Lee 21 S b.Lee) par. b. ----
   11 May, 1904, Lee

CUNDIFF

ROBT. (Lee 18 S frm b.Lee) par. b. Lee & Lee
   DONA LUCAS (Lee 23 S b.Lee) par. VA & Lee
   28 Feb., 1908 @ bride's home; aff. filed

DAMEREL

LARON (Lee 22 S frm b.--) par. b. ----
   ROSA ARNOLD (Wlf 23 S b.Lee) Lee, VA & Fay.
   7 May, 1903, Wolfe

DAVIS
ANDY (Lee 40 2nd "Cam.labor" b.Elliott) ----
    EVELYNE LITTLE (Lee 27 2nd b.Br.) Br. & Br.
    17 Sept., 1907, Beattyville, KY; aff. filed
GEORGE (Lee 21 S frm b.Lee) par. b. Lee & Lee
    SALLY COOMER (Lee 21 S b.Lee) par. b. ----
    25 Sept., 1907 @ bride's house; aff. filed
DAY
WALTER (Lee 22 S frm b.Lee) par. b. KY & KY
    MULARY COMBS (Lee 14 S b.--) par. b. ----
    24 Dec., 1902
DEATON
PRICE (Primrose 19 - frm b.Lee) par. Br. & Br.
    [Wm Price s/o Green Deaton & Sarah Spencer]
    HETTIE DEATON (Primrose 24 S b.Lee) par. b.
    Lee & Lee
    [d/o John Deaton & Nancy Marshall]
    7 Jan., 1910 @ residence [of] C. Creech
SHELDON (Filmore 22 S frm b.KY) par. KY & VA
    [s/o John Deaton & Nancy Marshall]
    ETTIE MORRIS (Filmore 18 S b.Lee) IN & Lee
    25 Aug., 1910 @ J. W. Morris'
WILLIAM PRICE (see PRICE)
DEERING
THOMAS (Red House 20 S RR b.KY) par. b. ----
    GINCEY TIPTON (Millers Cr. 20 S b.Lee) ---
    23 Aug., 1910 @ Clerk's office
DENNIS
BOONE (Lee 22 S frm b.Lee) par. Morg. & Lee
    LOU ELLEN HOGAN (Lee 17 S b.Lee) par. ----
    31 Oct., 1907 @ Andy Carter's; aff. filed
DUFF
LENORD (Lee 24 S frm b.--) par. b. ----
    EVA CAMBELL (Lee 25 2nd b.--) par. b. ----
    25 Nov., 1903, Lee
DUNAGAN
BERRY (Lee 21 S Tel.Op. b.Lee) par. b. ----
    ELLA TOLER (Lee 21 3rd b.Per.) par. b. ---
    11 Feb., 1904, Lee
GRANT (Lee 21 S RR b.Lee) par. b. ----
    DELILA RICHARDSON (Lee 16 S b.Est) par. ---
    3 Aug., 1904, Lee
HARLIN (Lee 19 S frm b.Lee) par. b. --- & Lee
    MARY ANGEL (Brown 19 S b.Lee) par.Lee & Lee
    24 Feb., 1910 @ Lewis Wregl's(?)

DUNAWAY
DAVID (Lee 28 2nd miner b.Lee) par. Ows. & Ows
    IDA PITMAN (Lee 20 S b.Lee) par. Est. & Est
    31 July, 1908, Beattyville
WILLIE (Lee 23 S RR b.Lee) par. Lee & Lee
    OLLIE ASHCRAFT (Lee 18 S b.Lee) par. b. ---
    24 Oct, 1907 @ James Durbin's; aff.filed
DURBIN
J. M. (Lee 22 S --- b.Lee) par. b. Est. & Est.
    LILLIE CARMACK (Lee 15 S b.Knox) Knox & Ows
    30 April, 1908 @ Co. Clk. office; aff filed
LUCIAN (Lee 25 S frm; b.--) par. b. ----
    ALICE SMITH (Lee 19 S b.--) par. b. ----
    29 Sept., 1903, Lee
LUSTER (Lee 20 S miner b.Lee) par. b. ----
    LIZZIE ROACH (Lee 21 S b.Lee) par. b. ----
    10 Nov., 1904, Lee

EDWARDS
JOHN (--- 21 S frm b.--) par. b. ----
    LUCY COMBS (Lee 17 S b.--) par. b. ----
    21 March, 1904, Lee
ENGLISH
WM. (Earnestv 22 S millman b.KY) par. KY & Lee
    LENA FARMER (Lee 22 S b.--) par. b. ----
    28 Dec., 1910 @ Bert Bowman's
ESTES
ANTHONY (Lee 22 S frm b.Lee) par. b. ----
    [s/o Wm. Estes & Laurinda Estes - RFR]
    SARAH C. SPARKS (Lee 16 S b.Jack.) par. ---
    8 Dec., 1904, Lee

FARGOT
ALEX (Jack. 21 S lab. b.KY) par. KY & Lee
    MINNIE GROSS (Br. 18 S b.KY) par. KY & KY
    15 Nov., 1910 @ Co. Clerk's office
FARMER
SIDNEY G. (Lee 18 S frm b.Lee) par. Lee & TN
    NELLIE MARCUM (Lee 18 S b.Ows.) Lee & Lee
    25 Dec., 1907 @ A. J. Marcum's; aff. filed
FIELDS
E. C. (Clay 37 2nd frm b.Per) par. Per. & Per.
    MARY BELLE TOLER (Lee 22 S b.Lee) Per & Lee
    5 Oct., 1907 @ J. Z(?) Parson's; aff. filed
JOHN (Lee 19 S RR b.Per.) par. b. ----
    MARY TYPTON (Lee 21 S b.NC) par. b. ----
    11 Oct., 1904, Lee

FLINCHUM
CHARLEY (Lee 24 S lab. b.--) par. b. ----
    ELLEN HUSTON (Lee 21 S b.--) par. b. ----
    27 Feb., 1904, Lee
J. B. (Lee 34 3rd crptr. b.Br.) par. Br. & Br.
    GERTRUDE COMBS (Lee 17 S b.Lee) Ows. & Lee
    12 Nov., 1907, Beattyville; aff. filed
FOUTS
HENRY (Lee 28 S frm b.Lee) par. b. ----
    MARSIE(?) DEATON (Lee 17 S b.Lee) par. ----
    28(?) June, 1904, Lee
FRALEY
JOHN (Lee 40 2nd lab. b.--) par. b. ----
    SALLIE B. MANN (Lee 18 S b.--) par. b. ----
    12 Nov., 1903, Lee
JOHN P. (Lee 21 S frm b.Lee) par. b. ----
    VIOLA MALONEY (Lee 16 S b.Lee) par. b. ----
    5 July, 1904, Lee

GABBARD
LOGAN (Lee 18 S frm b.--) par. b. ----
    FLORENCE M. BRANDENBURG (Lee 17 S b.--) ---
    21 Nov., 1903, Lee
GENTRY
ROBT. (Jack. 19 S teamster b.Est.) Est. & Est.
    BERTIE FARMER (Lee 18 S b.Lee) Lee & Lee
    13 Sept., 1907 @ bride's house; aff. filed
GILBERT
COLEMAN (Lee 19 S lumberman b.Lee) Lee & Lee
    MATTIE CARTER (Lee 21 S b.Lee) par b. ----
    29 March, 1908 @ D. Baker's; aff. filed
GOFORTH
HENRY C. (Lee 23 S crptr. b.Jack.) par. b. ---
    CLARA PORTER (Lee 17 S b.Lee) par. b. ----
    21 Nov., 1907 @ John Porter's; aff. filed
GOOD
RICHARD (Lee 38 2nd mining b.Rockc.) par. b.
    Rockc. & Rockc.
    REBECCA JANE FLINCHUM (Lee 32 2nd b.Lee)
    par. b. Lee & Br.
    6 Nov, 1907 @ Co. Clerk's office; aff.filed
GRANT
EDDA (E.Bernstet 22 S ---- b.Laurel) par. b.
    Laurel & Larlice(?), KY
    MATTIE CLUTS(?) (Idamay 22 S b.KY) KY & KY
    29 April, 1910 @ Co. Clerk's office

GROSS

CLIFTON (Br. 21 S mcht. b.Br.) par. Br. & Ows.
   LILLIAN CALAHAN (Br. 21 S b.Br.) Br. & Br.
   4 July, 1908 @ Pryse Hotel; aff. filed
LOUIS (Lee 22 S frm b.Br.) par. b. Br. & Lee
   NANCY JOHNSON (Lee 21 S b.Br.) Br. & Harl.
   17 Oct., 1907, Beattyville
ROBERT (Ows. 26 S frm b.--) par. b. ----
   MINNIE DAMERAL (Lee 20 S b.--) par. b. ----
   19 Oct., 1903, Lee
SAM (Lee 19 S frm b.Est.) par. b. ----
   SARAH B. MILLER (Lee 17 S b.Br.) par. ----
   22 Dec., 1904, Lee

HADDIX

CHARLEY (Lee 21 S miner b.Lee) par. Lee & Lee
   MAUD HOOTON(?) (Lee 16 S b.Lee) NC & Br.
   29 Jan., 1908 @ Bride's home; bride's
   father's affidavit

HALL

BROWNLOW (Lee 24 S b.Lee) par. b. Ows. & Ows.
   MAHELIA CONGLETON (Lee 23 S b.Lee) par. b.
   Ows. & Ows.
   - March, 1903, Lee
GEO. (Lee 21 S pub.wks. b.Harl.) Harl.& Harl.
   NANNIE(?) ESTES (Lee 16 S b.Lee) Lee & Lee
   30 July, 1908 @ Co. Clerk's office;
   bride's father's affidavit

HAMILTON

B. J. (Lee 31 3rd frm b.--) par. b. ----
   NORA GAY (Lee 21 S b.--) par. b. ----
   22 Dec., 1903, Lee
CHARLEY (Lee 19 S frm b.Lee) par. Per. & Br.
   DROISA(?) BURK (Lee 16 S b.Lee) par. b.
   Lee, VA & Lee, VA
   - Aug, 1903, Lee

HANN

O. A. (Lee 52 2nd frm b.--) par. b. ----
   ELLA HOGAN (Lee 37 2nd b.--) par. b. ----
   4 April, 1904, Lee

HARPER

CARL (OH 26 - frm b.OH) par. b. OH & OH
   MARTHA SEALE (Lee 36 S b.Ows.) MO(?) & TN
   12 June, 1910 @ W. H. Seale's

HARRISON
A. J. (Idamay 21 S miner b.Bell) Bell & ---
    LAURA SPIVA (Idamay 20 S b.Laurel) Br. & KY
    7 May, 1910 @ Geo. Spivey's
HATTON
BEN K. (Lee 23 S frm b.--) par. b. ----
    LILLIE NEWTON (Lee 23 S b.--) par. b. ----
    21 Oct., 1903, Lee
R. R. (Lee 46 6th lab. b.--) par. b. ----
    POLLY VAUGHN (Lee 22 2nd b.--) par. b. ---
    9 Nov., 1903, Lee
HAYES
CHAS. W (Beattyvl 17 S sch.tchr. b.KY) KY & KY
    JESSIE ALDRIDGE (Beattyvl. 21 S b.KY) par.
    b. KY & IN
    16 June, 1910 @ Presbyterian Church
HILL
KENLEE (St.Helens 22 S frm b.Lee) par. VA & VA
    ELISA SIMS (St.Helens 17 S b.Lee) Lee & Per
    10 March, 1910 @ C. L. Britton's
HOBBS
C. B. (Lee 26 S RR b.Lee) par. b. Ows. & ---
    CALLIE ABNER (Lee 25 S b.Lee) Ows. & Ows.
    2 April, 1903, Lee
HUGH (Ows. 21 S frm b.Jack.) par. b. -- & Clay
    LILLIE GABBARD (Lee 15 S b.Ows.) Clay & Br.
    22 Sept., 1907 @ H. T(?) Parson's; bride's
    father's affidavit
HOGAN
J. J. (Glanta, VA 26 S frm b.Glantan) VA & VA
    CARREY T(?) TYRE (Beattyvl. 23 S Laurel)
    par. b. KY & KY
    15 March, 1910
W. A. (IN 35 S frm b.IN) par. b. KY & KY
    ELIZA BRANSEN (Monica 18 S b.Lee) KY & KY
    20 April, 1910 @ W. H. Branson's
HORN
DUGLAS (Lee 23 S frm b.Lee) par. b. Ows. & Ows
    SERRA(?) D. DURBIN (Lee 20 S b.Lee) par. b.
    Ows. & Ows.
    3 June, 1903, Lee
WILBURN (Lee 21 S pub.wks. b.KY) par. KY & Lee
    GERTY FREEMAN (Lee 17 S b.KY) par. KY & KY
    20 Oct., 1910 @ Clerk's office

HOWELL
LAYFAYET (Lee 20 S frm b.Est) par. Est. & Est.
    LEANNA GROSS (Lee 14 S b.Br) par. Br. & Br.
    3 Oct., 1907 @ Ned Gross'; aff. filed
MITCHELL (Lee 23 S frm b.Lee) par. b. ----
    RUTH E. DURBIN (Lee 23 S b.Lee) par. b. ---
    17 Aug., 1904, Lee
HUMES
CLIFF (Lee 39 2nd miner b.Mad) par. Mad. & Mad
    LOUZY FOX (Lee 16 S b.Lee) par. Br. & Mad.
    14 June, 1908 @ Wm. Ewing's(?); aff. filed
    [per 1910 census, he is Blk. & she is Mul.]
HURST
NORBIN (Br. 21 S teacher b.Wlf.) par. b. ----
    PEARL ABNER (Lee 22 S b.Lee) par. b. ----
    20(?) July, 1904, Lee

ISAACS
W. P. (Lee 26 S frm b.Est.) par. b. ----
    CLEOPATRA BRANDENBURG (Lee 26 S b.Lee) ----
    29 Sept., 1904, Lee
ISOM
WILLIE (Lee 21 S porter b.Wlf) par. -- & Wlf.
    LAURA HAMPTON (Lee 22 S b.Lee) --- & Ows.
    27 May, 1908 @ Mint(?) Wilson's; both of
    age

JACKSON
SHELBY (Beattyvl. 28 S -- b.KY) par. KY & Lee
    MATTIE LEE FARLEY (Belle Pt. 28 S b.KY)
    par. b. KY & KY
    29 Dec., 1910 @ home of bride
JETT
CHAS. (Lee 25 S frm b.Br.) par. b. Br. & Br.
    JANE JETT (Lee 21 S b.Ows.) par. Ows. & Br.
    14 June, 1903, Ows.
JOHNSON
JEFF (Lee 27 S frm b.Lee) par. b. Wlf. & ---
    (bride unknown)
    - Jan., 1903, Lee
    [Though Margaret Dunaway was listed as his
    bride, the 1910 census puts her as the wf/o
    Milton Smith; see note under Milton Smith.]

JONES

J. M. (Lee 18 S lab. b.--) par. b. ----
    NANNIE ADAMS (Lee 21 S b.--) par. b. ----
    19 Sept., 1903, Lee
JOHN J (Lee 25 S frm b.Lee) par. Lee, VA & Ows
    LULA ARNOLD (Lee 21 S b.Lee) par. TN & Ows.
    27 June, 1908 @ bride's home
LESLIE (Lee 22 S frm b.Lee) par. b. ----
    DORA CREECH (Lee 21 S b.Lee) par. b. ----
    9 Sept., 1904, Lee

KELLY

HARUN(?) (Lee 21 "3rd" frm b.--) par. b. ----
    VISTA KINDRICK (Lee 17 S b.--) par. b. ----
    31 Dec., 1903, Lee
JOHN J. (-- 21 S frm b.--) par. b. ----
    JULA DUNAGIN (Lee 25 2nd b.--) par. b. ----
    21 March, 1904, Lee

KILBURN

LESLIE (Lee 18 S frm b.Lee) par. Br. & Lee
    LULA TIPTON (Lee 20 S b.Lee) par. Lee & Est
    5 Sept., 1907 @ bride's house; aff. filed

KINCAID

CHAS. (Fincastle 24 S frm b.Lee) par. KY & KY
    FLORENCE BARRETT (Beattyvl. 23 S b.Lee)
    par. b. Br. & Lee
    16 June, 1910 @ bride's house
DOUGLAS (Tallega 32 S bridgeman b.KY) KY & Lee
    MINNIE JOHNSON (Lee 24 S b.KY) par. KY & KY
    16 Nov., 1910 @ C. C. Johnson's
JACOB (Lee 24 S lumberman b.Lee) Ows. & Ows.
    ALICE E. SMYTH (Lee 25 S b.Lee) VA & Ows.
    1 July, 1908 @ bride's home
MELVIN (Lee 25 S frm b.Lee) par. Ows. & Ows.
    LUCINDA CABLE (Lee 23 S b.Wlf) par. b.
    Lee Co., VA & VA
    26 Feb., 1908 @ Whig Cable's

KING

JOHN (Beattyvl. 21 S miner b.Knox) Knox & Knox
    MAY SMITH (Beattyvl. 17 S b.Beattyvl.) par.
    b. Br. & Br.)
    16 July, 1910, St. Helens @ B. Smith's
KOWLEN(?) [NOLEN?]

ANDERSON (Lee 23 S frm b.Ows.) Ows. & Ows.
    MARY TURNER (Lee 16 S b.--) par. KY & KY
    29 March, 1910 @ R. L. Turner's

LAMBERT
A. S. (-- 32 S frm b.KY) par. b. KY & KY
    DORA HAMELTON (Lee 19 S b.Est) Jack. & Jack
    20 March, 1903, Lee
LANDERS(?)
GILBERT (Jess. 22 S frm b.Jess) par. Mad & Mad
    IBBIE MOPPIN (Ows. 18 S b.Ows.) par. ----
    24 Dec., 1907, Beattyville, KY; aff. filed
LAUTER(?)
ELMER C. (Mad. 22 2nd crptr. b.OH) par. b.
    Mad. & Laurel
    LOTTIE THOMPSON (Lee 16 S b.Lee) par. ----
    31 March, 1908 @ Louisa Thompson's; bride's
    mother's affidavit
LAWSON
J. G. (Lee 23 S frm b.Wlf.) par. b. Wlf. & VA
    LUCY McINTOSH (Lee 20 S b.Lee) Ows. & --
    15 Feb., 1910 @ Thos. McIntosh's
JOHN (Lee 21 S frm b.Wlf.) par. b. Wlf. & NC
    MAGGIE LAWSON (Lee 15 S b.Wlf) par.TN & Lee
    21 Nov., 1907 @ Wm. Lawson's; aff. filed
ROBT. (Lee 24 S frm b.Wlf.) par. Wlf. & Wlf.
    REBECCA MOORE (Lee 16 S b.Ows.) Ows. & --
    5 Dec., 1907 @ Wm. Moore's; aff. filed
W. H. (Lee 21 S frm b.Menf) par. b. Br. & Br.
    ALLIE BENNETT (Ows. 15 S b.Beattyvl.) par.
    b. Ows. & Ows.
    11 Aug., 1910 @ Wm. "Barrett's"
LEMASTER
KEEN (Beattyvl 48 2nd pub.wks. b.John.) par.
    b. John. & John.
    LIZZIE STAMPER (Lee 23 S b.Lee) par. ----
    7 May, 1908 @ J. A. Stamper's; aff. filed
LUCAS
DECORSEY (Lee 23 S frm b.Lee) par. Lee & Lee
    ANNIE LUTES (Lee 21 S b.Lee) par. Lee & Lee
    21 April, 1908 @ bride's home; aff. filed
HARRISON (Lee 21 S Tel.Op. b.Lee) Lee & ---
    CORELA DANEL [DANIEL?] (Monica 18 S b.Lee)
    par. b. Lee & Est.
    6 June, 1910 @ W. C. Danell's
HENRY P. (Lee 24 S lab. b.Boyd) par. b. ----
    EMILY STAMPER (Lee 15 S b.Carter) par. ----
    20 April, 1904, Lee

LUDFORD
WM. (Lee 23 S lawyer b.Lee) par. Lee & Lee
    NETTIE SMITH (Lee 16 S b.Lee) Lee & Ows.
    13 Sept., 1907 @ bride's house; aff. filed
LUTES
LOT (Lee 23 S miner b.Lee) par. b. Lee & Lee
    NANNIE LETHGOE (Lee 15 S b.Laurel) par. b.
    Knox(?) & TN
    25 Dec, 1907 @ Luther Lethgoe's; bride's
    father's affidavit
LYNCH
WALTER (Lee 22 S frm b.--) par. b. ----
    KATE HAMILTON (Lee 16 S b.--) par. b. ----
    10 March, 1904, Lee

McCALL
PETE (Lee 28 S timberman b.Pow.) par. OH & Pow
    GLADIS INGRAM (Lee 16 S Menf.) Bath & Wlf.
    6 Sept., 1907 @ bride's house; aff. filed
McGUIRE
HENRY (Beattyvl 27 S lawyer b.KY) par.KY & Lee
    LOLA MORRAN (Lex. 22 S b.KY) par. KY & KY
    14 Dec., 1910, Maysfield, KY
JAMES B. (Lee 27 S frm b.--) par. b. ----
    NETTIE O. WHEELER (Lee 26 S b.--) par. ----
    7 Dec., 1903, Lee
LIN (St.Helens 38 S lab. b.Lee) par. Ows & Ows
    [s/o John Warwick McGuire & Cath. Akers]
    LILLIE BRANDENBERG (St.Helens 22 S b.Lee)
    par. b. Ows. & Ows.
    27 Aug., 1910 @ bride's house
McKINNEY
SAMUEL C. (Lee 27 2nd frm b.Est.) par. b. ----
    MARY ETTA ROBINSON (Lee 22 S b.Est) NC & NC
    7 March, 1908 @ Widow(?) Robertson's;
    affidavit filed
McQUINN/McQUIN
C. T. (Wlf. 29 S frm b.Wlf.) par. Wlf. & Wlf.
    ANNIE BARRETT (Lee 22 S b.Lee) par. Br & Br
    27 Aug, 1908 @ Jack Barrett's
J. F. (Lee 30 S RR b.Morg) par. b. Morg. & Ows
    SARAH McDANIEL (Lee 19 S b.Knott) Br. & Per
    10 April, 1908 @ A. McDaniel's; bride's
    father's affidavit

101

MANN
SID (Lee 41 2nd frm b.Lee) par. b. ----
    MAGGIE COUCH (Lee 21 S b.Ows.) par. b. ----
    15 Oct., 1904, Lee
MARCUM
ALBERT(?) (Lee 20 S Tel.Op. b.--) par. b. ----
    CALLIE BRANDENBURG (Lee 16 S b.--) par. ---
    4 Feb., 1904, Lee
MAYS
HARRISON (Tallega 21 S frm b.Lee) par.KY & Lee
    LILLIE MILLER (Idamay 18 S b.KY) Br. & KY
    1 Oct., 1910 @ J. E. Miller's
JOHN (Lee 25 S frm b.Lee) par. b. ----
    NANNIE JONES (Lee 20 S b.Lee) par. b. ----
    25 Aug., 1904, Lee
PRICE (Banford 19 S frm b.Lee) par. Ows. & Ows
    EMILY BELLMAN (Lee 20 S b.Br.) Per. & --
    5 Feb., 1910 @ John Thomas'
WHITLEY (Lee 20 S frm b.Lee) par. b. ----
    LILLIE FARMER (Lee 16 S b.Lee) par. b. ----
    22 Dec., 1904, Lee
MEADOWS
CHARLEY (Lee 38 2nd frm b.Est) par. Est. & Est
    EMILY SAMPLES (Lee 29 S b.VA) par. VA & --
    25 Dec., 1907 @ Sarah Samples'; aff. filed
J. D. (Wlf. 35 3rd B'smith b.Pow.) Pow. & Est.
    MOLLIE JONES (Lee 17 S b.Est) par. VA & Est
    6 Sept., 1907 @ bride's house; bride's
    father's affidavit
MEYERS
W. T. (Lee 25 S lab. b.Montg.) par. b. ----
    FLORENCE WILSON (Lee 22 S b.Allen Co.) ----
    25 Dec., 1903, Lee
MILLER
GEORGE (Lee 21 S frm b.Lee) par. Ows. & ---
    MARTHA COLE (Lee 16 S b.Lee) par. Ows. & TN
    26 March, 1903, Lee
MINTER
Joe (Monica 20 S frm b.Lee) par. b. Br. & KY
    LOTTIE WHITE (Tallega 20 S b.Lee) Lee & Lee
    9 Sept., 1910 @ Grant White's
MOORE
RILEY (Lee 23 S frm b.Jack.) par. Jack. & Jack
    GEORGIA COMBS (Filmore 17 S b.Lee) par. b.
    Per. & Per.
    9 March, 1910 @ Arminia Combs'

NEWMAN
H. H. (Lee 29 2nd --- b.Lee) par. b. ----
    MARY J. STEPP (Lee 26 2nd b.Lee) par. ----
    29 Dec., 1904, Lee
HENRY (Lee 21 S frm b.--) par. b. ----
    NETTIE MAYS (Lee 18 S b.--) par. b. ----
    17 Sept., 1903, Lee
ROBERT (Lee 22 S teacher b.Lee) par. b. ----
    OLLIE GABARD (Lee 18 S b.Lee) par. b. ----
    25 Aug., 1904, Lee
S. P(?) (Lee 30 2nd frm b.Lee) par. b. ----
    ROSA L. BANKS (Lee 16 S b.Clay) par. ----
    29 Aug., 1904, Lee
NORMAN
GRANT (Lee 22 S Tel.Op. b.--) par. b. ----
    NANNIE MARSHALL (Lee 22 S b.--) par. ----
    4 Feb., 1904, Lee
L. C. JR. (Beattyvl. 31 S Mine Op. b.KY) par.
    b. Boone & Boone
    EMILY COCKERELL (Beattyvl. 24 2nd b.Lee)
    par. b. Lee & Br.
    8 Jan., 1910, Beattyville, KY

O'CONNOR
GREEN (Br. 26 S "Cam.Labor" b.Br.) Ire. & Br.
    [s/o Mike O'Connor & Ursula Jane Hays] RWO
    DAISEY COOMER (Lee 18 S b.Lee) Adair & ---
    26 Sept, 1907 @ bride's house; father's aff
OLIVER
GEORGE (Idamay 21 S miner b.KY) par. KY & Lee
    LENA COLE (Lee 17 S b.KY) par. b. KY & KY
    9 Dec., 1910 @ Price Cole's
OWSLEY
JESSE (Lee 29 S frm b.Est.) par. b. ----
    SOPHIA STAMPER (Lee 29 2nd b.Est.) par. ---
    28 July, 1904, Lee

PALMER/PARMER
JOHN (Lee 19 S frm b.Ows.) par. b. Lee & Ows.
    DORA BOWMAN (Lee 14 S b.Ows) par. Ows. & Br
    14 June, 1903, Ows.
JOHN H. (Lee 19 S frm b.Lee) par. Ows. & Br.
    HULDA BOWMAN (Ows. 16 S b.Lee) Ows. & Br.
    24 Feb., 1903, Ows.
WALKER (Tallega 22 S frm b.KY) par. KY & Lee
    ANNA McINTOSH (Athol 18 S b.KY) KY & KY
    20 Oct., 1910 @ Green Kilburn's

PARSONS
ZION (Lee 24 S frm b.Lee) par. b. VA & Lee
    KITTIE ALLEN (Lee 21 S b.Clay) Clay & Wlf.
    12 Oct., 1907 @ bride's home; aff. filed
PENCE
JOAB (Wlf. 22 S frm b.Wlf.) par. Wlf. & Wlf.
    VINEY BRANS (Evelyn 18 S b.Lee) par. b.
    Laurel & Ows.
    14 July, 1910 @ Emery Bartlett's
NEWTON (Lee 33 2nd frm b.Wlf) par. Wlf. & Wlf.
    DORA COMBS (Wlf. 30 2nd b.Wlf) Wlf. & Wlf.
    11 July, 1910, Brown, KY
PHILLIPS
CLEVELAND (Lee 20 S miner b.Lee) par. b. ----
    BERTHA ROACH (Lee 19 S b.Lee) par. b. ----
    22 Sept., 1904, Lee
GEO. (Lee 20 S frm b.Wlf.) par. Montg. & Wlf.
    BESSIE LEMASTER (Lee 14 S b.Elliott Co.)
    par. b. Morg. & Elliott
    30 Nov, 1907 @ Spence Lemaster's; aff.filed
PITMAN
CHAS. (Lee 31 S lab. b.--) par. b. ----
    LIZIE JOHNSON (Lee 17 S b.--) par. b. ----
    5 Nov., 1903, Lee
JESSE (Lee 25 S miner b.Lee) par. b. ----
    LILLIE SCHULL (Lee 16 S b.Lee) par. b. ----
    8 Nov., 1904, Lee
M. C. (Lee 30 S lab. b.Lee) par. b. ----
    LILLIE A. BLEVINS (Lee 16 S b.Ows.) -----
    21 May, 1904, Lee
POWELL
J. D. (Lee 42 2nd B'smth b.--) par. b. ----
    ELIZA McGUIRE (Lee 29 2nd b.--) par. ----
    5 Nov., 1903, Lee
PRICE
BRACK (Ows. 21 S frm b.Ows.) par. Ows. & Lee
    OLLIE BELLE FRISBEY (Lee 16 S b.Laurel)
    par. b. Menf. & TN
    4 June, 1908 @ J. E. Dunigan's; bride's
    father's affidavit
JOHN (Lee 21 S frm b.Ows.) par. b. ----
    MARTHA STAMPER (Lee 19 S b.Lee) par. ----
    12 May, 1904, Lee
THOMAS (Lee 23 S frm b.Lee) par. b. ----
    LUCINDA DUNAWAY (Lee 17 S b.Lee) par. ----
    22 Dec., 1904, Lee

PRITCHARD
JOHN (Lee 22 S frm b.Lee) par. b. ----
    CALLIE J. KELLY (Lee 22 S b.Lee) par. ----
    1 June, 1904, Lee
PROFITT
H. F. (Lee 20 S frm b.Wlf.) par. b. ----
    LELLA SMITH (Lee 20 S b.Lee) par. b. ----
    3 Aug., 1904, Lee

QUILLEN
HARLAN (Lee 27 S mcht. b.Lee) par. VA & Ows.
    MYRTIE CONGLETON (Lee 20 S b.Lee) Lee & Lee
    7 May, 1908 @ bride's home; bride's
    father's affidavit
QUINTON
OLIVER (Idamay 25 S miner b.KY) par. KY & Lee
    MATTIE "SPRAY" (Lee 18 S b.KY) par. KY & KY
    3 Dec., 1910 @ Geo. Spivey's

RADER
ALBERT (Lee 23 2nd "Cam.Labor" b.Jack.) par.
    b. Lee & Jack.
    JOSIE ADDISON (Lee 22 S b.Ows.) Lee & Ows.
    22 Oct., 1907 @ Isaac Addison's
JOHN M. (Lee 25 S frm b.--) par. b. ----
    AMANDA BOAZ (Lee 16 S b.--) par. b. ----
    7 April, 1904, Lee
JOSEPH (Lee 23 2nd pub.wks b.Jack.) Lee & ---
    AMANDA BOWLES (Est. 19 2nd b.Est.) par. ---
    16 Sept., 1907, Beattyville, KY; aff. filed
REESE
LUCIAN (Lee 20 S frm b.--) par. b. ----
    SARAH J. TIREY (Lee 18 S b.--) par. b. ----
    10 Dec., 1903, Lee
RICHARDSON
LEN(?) (Lee 21 S RR b.Est) par. b. Est. & Est.
    SARAH DEATON (Lee 18 S b.Lee) par.Lee & Lee
    [d/o John Deaton & Nancy Marshall]
    2 Sept., 1907 @ bride's house; bride's
    father's affidavit
RILEY
JOHN D. (Lee 20 S frm b.--) par. b. ----
    ZERANEY DURBIN (Lee 19 S b.--) par. b. ----
    6 Oct., 1903, Lee

ROACH
GEORGE (Lee 23 S frm b.Lee) par. b. Per. & Br.
    ANNIE BARRUS(?) (Lee 19 S b.Lee) par. b.
    Br. & Lee(?)
    ---------?, 1903, Lee
ROBERTS
LOGAN (Lee 20 S miner b.Lee) par. b. ----
    CLARA BATES (Lee 15 S b.Lee) par. NC & Lee
    10 April, 1908 @ John Bates'; aff. filed
ROGERS
CHARLEY (Est. 25 S pub.wks. b.Est) Est. & Est.
    VIOLA McQUEEN (Lee 18 2nd b.Lee) Lee & Lee
    21 Sept., 1907 @ Joe Abner's; aff. filed
ROSE
ASA (Lee 22 S Tel.Op. b.--) par. b. ----
    CALLIE McGUIRE (Lee 19 S b.--) par. b. ----
    2 Feb., 1904, Lee
ROSS
GREEN B. (Lee 24 S frm b.Ows.) par. b. ----
    EDNA BRANDENBURG (Lee 19 S b.Lee) par. ----
    22 Oct., 1904, Lee
ROWE
CLINT (Lee 20 S miner b.Laurel) Laurel & Jack.
    SARAH MARSHAL (Lee 23 2nd b.Br.) par. ----
    25 Aug., 1908 @ Co. Judge's office; aff.
    filed
ROWLAND
THOS. W. (Lee 23 S pub.wks. b.Ows) Ows. & Ows.
    LOURETTA METCALF (Lee 16 S b.Jack.) par. b.
    Jack. & Jack.
    30 July, 1908 @ James Metcalf's; aff. filed

SAMS
J. M. (Pebworth 23 S crptr. b.Lee) Clay & Lee
    FANNY SHANKS (Lee 17 S b.Lee) Ows. & Lee
    3 March, 1910 @ Tilman Shanks'
SHAFFER
CLARENCE (Lee 22 S lumberman b.Hardin) par. b.
    Green(?) & VA
    KATE HALL (Lee 17 S b.Lee) par. Lee & Lee
    18 Dec., 1907 @ bride's home; aff. filed
SHEARER
LUCIEN (Lee 24 S frm b.Montg) par. Lee & Montg
    DELILA WILLIAMS (Lee 17 2nd b.Lee) Lee & VA
    29 Jan., 1908 @ H. Williams'; aff. filed

SHOEMAKER
ENOS(?) (Lee 22 S frm b.Lee) par. b. ----
    CORDELIA COMBS (Lee 17 S b.Lee) par. b. ---
    23 June, 1904, Lee
HIRAM (Lee 19 S frm b.Lee) par. b. ----
    SALLIE STAMPER (Lee 29 S b.Per.) par. ----
    25 Aug., 1904, Lee
WILLIAM R. (--- 32 2nd frm b.Lee) par. b. ----
    LORATTE SMITH (Lee 17 S b.Lee) par. b. ----
    16 March, 1904, Lee
SHORT
ASA (Lee 29 2nd frm b.--) par. b. ----
    ARZELLA WHITE (Lee 29 2nd b.--) par. b. ---
    27(?) Jan., 1904, Lee
SIMMS(?)
J. R. (Lee 25 S messenger b.Mad) par.Mad & Mad
    KATHALENE SUTTON (Lee 17 S b.Lee) TN & Ows.
    11 Dec., 1907, Versailes; bride's father's
    affidavit
SIMS
JOHN (Beattyvl. 31 2nd crptr. b.Proctor) -----
    BETIE SHOUSE (Beattyvl. 21 S b.Beattyvl)
    par. b. KY & KY
    7 May, 1910, Beattyville
SLOAN
CLEM (Br. 27 S lab. b.Lee) par. b. ----
    MATTIE MALAYER (Lee 27 S b.Lee) par. b. ---
    9 July, 1904, Lee
ROLLA (Beattyvl. 21 S lab. b.KY) par. KY & Lee
    HARAH PHILLIPS (Lee 16 S b.KY) par. KY & KY
    26 Nov., 1910 @ John Lyons'
SMITH
CHAS. G. (Est. 22 S frm b.Est) par. Ows. & Est
    MAGGIE NEWTON (Lee 16 S b.Lee) Ows. & Ows.
    10 Dec., 1902, Lee
DUDLY (Radical 27 2nd frm b.KY) par. KY & Lee
    ANNA PROFFITT (Radical 15 S b.KY) KY & KY
    1 Dec., 1910 @ Christney Proffitt's
EMMITT (Lee 28 2nd frm b.Ows.) par. b. Lee Co,
    VA & ---
    MATTIE FARMER (Lee 26 2nd b.Lee) Ows. & Lee
    1 Oct., 1907 @ bride's home; aff. filed
ENOCH (Proctor 32 S frm b.KY) par. b. KY & Lee
    EMILY FIELDS (Lee 32 2nd b.--) par. ----
    24 Dec., 1910 @ home of bride

SMITH (cont.)
JOHN N. (Lee 48 2nd mcht. b.Ows.) par. b. ---
    CORDELIA DICKERSON (Lee 28 S b.Lee) par. --
    27 Aug., 1904, Lee
MATT (Lee 18 S frm b.Lee) par. Ows. & Ows.
    FANNIE DAMEREL (Lee 19 S b.Lee) Ows. & Ows.
    - Aug., 1903, Lee
M[ILTON] H. (Lee 58 2nd frm b.Ows) Ows. & Est.
    MARGARET DUNAWAY (Lee 49 3rd b.Ows.) par.
    Ows. & Ows.
    - April, 1903
    [NOTE: Though no bride was listed for
    Milton, the 1910 census shows that his wife
    was Margaret age 50; she was the bride
    listed for Jeff Johnson (age 27), the next
    groom on the page. Margaret was appar. md.
    to a Tincher at one time, because Tincher
    stepchildren are listed w/them 1910.]
ROBERT R. (Lee 18 S frm b.Lee) par. b. ----
    NORA TINCHER (Lee 21 S b.Lee) par. b. ----
    23 July, 1904, Lee
TAULBY (Lee 23 S mcht. b.Lee) par. Ows. & Ows.
    LILLIE GRAY (Lee 24 S b.Lee) par. Lee & Ows
    23 April, 1908 @ Wm. Gray's
SNOWDEN
ENOS (Lee 31 S frm b.Lee) par. b. Lee & Lee
    OLLIE SPARKS (Lee 21 S b.Lee) Est. & Lee
    5 Feb., 1908 @ Wm. Gray's
SPARKS
SAMUEL (Est. 25 S frm b.Est.) par. Est. & Est.
    ALICE HOWELL (Lee 16 S b.Lee) Est. & Est.
    19 Dec., 1907 @ bride's house; aff. filed
SPENCE
FRANK (Ows. 23 S frm b.Ows.) par. b. ----
    EDNIE CORNETT (Lee 17 S b.Lee) par. ----
    13 Oct., 1904, Lee
HENRY C. (Ows. 34 S miller b.Lee) VA & Lee
    FLORENCE MARCUM (Lee 17 S b.--) par. ----
    10 Aug., 1910 @ A. J. Marcum's
SPICER
BERRY (Lee 25 S frm b.--) par. b. ----
    RODA LEGG (Lee 23 S b.--) par. b. ----
    19 Sept., 1903, Lee
STACY
BRECK (Lee 21 S frm b.--) par. b. ----
    LILLIE M. JEWELL (Lee 16 S b.--) par. ----
    21 Sept, 1903, Lee

STAFFORD
WILLIE (Lee 19 S RR b.Lee) par. b. OH & Pow.
    MARIAH WALTON (Lee 17 S b.---) par. ----
    24 Dec., 1907 @ George Walton's; aff. filed
STAMPER
BURTON (Millers Cr. 20 S frm b.KY) KY & Lee
    ELLIE LUCAS (Monica 21 S b.KY) par. KY & KY
    24 Dec, 1910 @ Jno. Lucas'
EMANUEL (Evelyn 24 S miner b.Br) par. Br. & --
    [s/o Peter Stamper & Mary Stamper]
    VINA MAYS (Evelyn 21 S b.Lee) Br. & Br.
    19 May, 1910, Levi, KY
ENOCH (Lee 49 3rd frm b.Br.) par. b. ----
    MARGRETT DAMERAL (Lee 44 3rd b.Lee) ----
    23 Nov., 1904, Lee
GROVER (Lee 22 S frm b.Lee) par. Ows. & Pow.
    [s/o Joseph & Martha Stamper]
    OLLIE COMBS (Lee 17 S b.Clk) par. Br. & Br.
    3 June, 1908 @ bride's home; aff. filed
HUSTON (Wlf. 21 S frm b.Wlf) par. Wlf. & Per.
    CARRIE M. KINCAID (Lee 17 S b.Lee) par. b.
    Ows. & Ows.
    21 May, 1903, Lee
W. C. (OK 38 2nd frm b.Wlf) par. b. Wlf. & Wlf
    ELIZA ARNOLD (Lee 32 S b.Lee) par. Lee & VA
    7 Feb., 1908 @ N. J. Arnold's; aff. filed
W. O. B. (Lee 58 3rd frm b.Ows.) par. NC & VA
    MARANDA TAYLOR (Lee 38 2nd b.Wlf) Wlf & Wlf
    26 May, 1908 @ W.O.B. Stamper's; aff. filed
STEELE
J. W. (Lee 21 S sawmilling b.Lee) Lee & Lee
    OMEGA ROBINSON (Lee 18 S b.Montg.) par. b.
    Ows. & Ows.
    25 Dec., 1907 @ Wm. Robinson's; aff. filed
STEPHENS
BERT (Lee 21 S frm b.Est.) par. b. Est. & --
    LAURA McKENEY (Lee 19 S b.Lee) Est. & Est.
    30 April, 1908 @ Co. Clerk's office; aff.
    filed
STIDHAM
JAMES L (Jack. 28 2nd policeman b.Br) Br. & Br
    [s/o Andrew J. Stidham & Nancy A. Davidson]
    CALLIE F. STAMPER (Lee 21 2nd b.Jack.) par.
    b. Wlf. & Ows.
    6 Feb., 1908 @ bride's home

STRANBURY
GEORGE (Louisvl. 28 S brid[ge]man b.Louisvl.)
    par. b. MD & MD
    LULA NEWMAN (Lee 16 S b.Lee) par. Ows & Lee
    20 Feb., 1908, Heidelburg; aff. filed
STRONG
A. J. (Br. 28 S frm b.Br.) par. b. ----
    LYDIE CREECH (Lee -- 2nd b.Lee) par. ----
    3 Dec., 1904, Lee
SWAN
JOHN F. (Heidleburg 24 S "Pebworth" b.IN) par.
    b. Ows. & Lee [NOTE: Pebworth is a town]
    NANNIE "SHACK" (Lee 24 S b.Lee) Lee & ---
    30 May, 1910 @ Tilman Shanks
SWEENEY
CURT (Br. 21 2nd frm b.Wlf.) par. b. VA & Wlf.
    LENA LUTES (Lee 21 S b.Lee) par. Lee & Lee
    18 June, 1908 @ Ella Lutes'

THACKER
ELISHA (Lee 28 S frm b.--) par. b. ----
    MARTHA SMITH (Lee 18 S b.--) par. b. ----
    3 Dec., 1903, Lee
THOMAS
GARFIELD (Lee 25 2nd RR b.Lee Co., VA) ----
    SARAH BOWMAN (Lee 27 S b.Mercer) Ows. & --
    13 Feb., 1908 @ Ben Coomer's; aff. filed
JAMES (Torrent 21 S RR b.KY) par. b. KY & Lee
    JOSIE PARSONS (Lee 21 S b.KY) par. KY & KY
    16 Oct., 1910 @ Emily Parsons'
SAMUEL (Lee 41 S frm b.Lee) par. b. Lee & Lee
    IDA BRANDENBURG (Lee 22 S b.Lee) Lee & Br.
    9 March, 1910 @ Houstin Brandenburg's
TINCHER
W. H. (Lee 29 S miner b.Lee) par. b. ----
    MARTHA EVANS (Lee 28 S b.Lee) par. b. ----
    22 May, 1904, Lee
TIPTON
MILLARD (Pryse 24 S frm b.KY) par. b. KY & Lee
    MAGGIE LANE (Fincastle 18 S b.KY) KY & KY
    28 Dec., 1910 @ home of bride
TOLER
LOGAN (Lee 22 S lab. b.Lee) par. b. ----
    VINA MILLER (Lee 18 S b.Lee) par. b. ----
    24 Dec., 1903, Lee

TOWNSEND
JOHN (Belle Pt. 74 2nd frm b.Est.) Est. & Est.
    LUCY JANE COLE (Belle Pt. 40 2nd b.Lee)
    par. b. Ows. & Ows.
    5 Aug., 1910 @ Co. Clerk's office
TREADWAY
ARCH (Lee 25 S frm b.Lee) par. b. Lee & Lee
    EVA THOMAS (Lee 23 S b.Lee) par. Lee & Ows.
    5 Feb., 1908 @ bride's home; aff. filed
BASCOM (Lee 22 S Erie Engineering? b.Ows.)
    par. b. Ows. & VA
    ROSA JONES (Lee 16 S b.Lee) par. Lee & Lee
    13 Feb., 1908, Heidelburg, KY
SAM (Lee 24 S frm b.Morg.) par. b. Lee & Est.
    ADDIE MAY SHACKELFORD (Lee 24 S b.Lee) par.
    b. Wlf. & Lee
    25 Dec., 1907, Beattyville "Juc"
TRENT
BEN (Lee 22 S porter b.KY) par. b. Linc. & --
    POLLY CRAWFORD (Lee 21 S b.Lee) par. b. ---
    17 April, 1908 @ Mack Sewell's; both of age
TURNER
-----? (Lee 24 S frm b.Lee) par. b. Per. & Br.
    ----------? (Ows. 17 S b.Ows) Ows. & Lee(?)
    -----?, 1902/3(?), Lee
-----? (Lee 22 S frm b.Lee) par. b. Per. & Br.
    -----? STAMPER (Ows. 17 S b.Lee) par. b.
    Br. & Lee(?)
    -----?, 1902/3(?), Lee
JOHN D. (Lee 24 S pub.wks. b.Lee) par. Br & Br
    MOLLIE PLOWMAN (Lee 16 S b.Lee) par. ----
    24 Dec., 1907 @ D. Turner's; aff. filed
SILAS (Lee 19 S frm b. KY) par. b. KY & Lee
    BETTIE SMITH (Lee 15 S b.--) par. b. ----
    25 Dec., 1910 @ J. P. Smith's
TURRELL
JOSEPH C. (Leighton 36 2nd lab. b.--) par. ---
    MARTHA F. YOUNG (Lee 29 2nd b.KY) KY & KY
    20 Dec., 1910 @ Dave Young's
TYPTON
CHAS. F. (Lee 32 S frm b.--) par. b. ----
    EMILY OLINGER (Lee 32 2nd b.--) par. b. ---
    11 April, 1904, Lee

TYREE
C. G. (Mad. 22 S conductor b.Est.) par. b. ---
  SALLY MAY TURPIN (Louisvl. 21 S b.Breck.)
  par. b. ----
  7 Sept., 1907 @ Lee But------?; aff. filed

UPTHEGROVE(?)
OLIA (Lee 21 S operator b.Linc.) Linc. & Linc.
  NETTIE EVANS (Lee 17 S b.Lee) par. b. ----
  9 Oct, 1907 @ Co. Clerk's office; aff.filed

VANDERPOOL
E. D. (Lee 29 S RR b.Lee) par. b. ----
  POLINA TOLER (Lee 26 2nd b.Lee) par. b. ---
  2 July, 1904, Lee

WADE
MILLARD (Lee 21 S frm b.Lee) par. b. ----
  MARGRETT TINCHER (Lee 15 S b.Lee) par. ---
  12 Oct., 1904, Lee
WILLIAM (Lee 26 S frm b.Lee) par. b. ----
  GEORGE A. FIKE (Lee 23 2nd b.Lee) par. ----
  25 Aug., 1904, Lee
WARD
CHARLEY (Ows. 24 S frm b.Shelby) Jack. & Jack.
  CONNIE BURKE (Lee 18 S b.Ows.) par. VA & VA
  7 Oct., 1907 Pryse House; aff. filed
WARNER
JEFF (Lee 31 S frm b.Lee) par. b. Ows. & Ows.
  LUCY SMALLWOOD (Lee 32 3rd b.Lee) Ows & Ows
  - April, 1903, Lee
WARWICK
WM. (Idamay 29 S miner b.Lee) par. b. TN & KY
  GRACE QUINTER (Idamay 19 S b.Lee) Lee & Lee
  10 Sept., 1910 @ W. H. Quinter's
WEAR
ANDELE J. (Banford 21 S frm b.Clk) Clk. & Clk.
  MARY J DURBIN (Banford 18 S b.Lee) Est & TN
  19 Feb., 1910 @ Hade Durbin's
WILLIAMS
CLEVELAND (Lee 22 S frm b.Lee) par. Br. & Br.
  MILLIE SPICER (Lee 15 S b.Br.) Br. & Lee
  6 Aug., 1908 @ bride's home; father's aff.
ELIJA[H] (Lee 38 3rd frm b.Per.) par. b. ----
  LAURA HAYS (Lee 22 S b.Wlf.) par. b. ----
  24 Dec., 1904, Lee

WILLIAMS (cont.)
JOSEPH (Lee 21 S frm b.Est.) par. b. ----
    POLINA FAULKNER (Lee 21 S b.Lee) par. ----
    8 Oct., 1904, Lee
WILLIEN
HENSON (Idamay 25 S miner b.Lee) Lee & Lee
    ALLEY MAY FOURBIN (Idamay 16 S b.KY) par.
    b. KY & KY
    17 Sept., 1910, Idamay
WILOBY
CRAXTON (Lee 21 S frm b.Montg.) par. b. ----
    ADA CONKWRIGHT (Lee 18 S b.Montg.) par. ---
    5 Nov., 1904, Lee
WILSON
BARNIE (Lee -- S ---- b.Lee) par. b. Lee & Lee
    KATIE BEACH (Lee -- S b.Lee) par. Lee & Lee
    - Dec., 1902, Lee
RELLIE (Lee -- S ---- b.--) par. b. ----
    MAUD DAVIS (Lee 19 S b.Ows.) Ows. & Lee, VA
    11 Sept., 1903, Lee
WIRES
BAILEY (OK 19 S frm b.OK) par. b. KS & OK
    RACHEL LUCAS (Lee 19 S b.Lee) Lee & Lee
    15 May, 1908 @ bride's home; aff. filed
WITT
PRICE (Heidleburg 24 2nd frm b.Lee) par. b.
    Lee Co., VA & Ows.
    LIZZIE GIBS (Heidleburg 22 S b.Wlf) par.
    b. Wlf. & Wlf.
    24 Jan., 1910 @ John Gibs'
WOOSLEY
JAMES (Lee 23 S frm b.Est.) par. Pow. & Est.
    FRANKIE STAMPER (Lee 17 S b.Lee) Lee & Lee
    6 June, 1908 @ bride's home; aff. filed
WRIGHT
MOSES (Banford 24 S frm b.Lee) par. Lee & Lee
    ELIZABETH KENDRICKS (Banford 19 S b.Lee)
    par. b. Lee & Per.
    - March, 1910

YORK
ROBT. L. (Lee 35 2nd mining b.Lee) Lee & Br.
    CILLA MANN (Lee 21 2nd b.Lee) Est. & Lee
    14 Nov., 1907 @ Mart Charles'

YOUNG
SAMUEL (Lee 25 S Lum.Insp. b.Linc.) par. ----
    ODA WHITE (Lee 25 S b.OH) par. b. ----
    20 April, 1904, Lee

INDEX

[NOTE: For the most part, I have not listed any middle initials in the index.]

* = listed more than once on a page

(surnames unreadable)
-------?
  ------? (fem) - 111
-----HIRTS(?)
  -----? (fem) - 68
-----RBLE(?)
  Rollie - 83

ABNER
  Amelia Ann - 1, 41   Martha - 38
  Buck - 83   Nannie - 85
  Callie - 97   Pearl - 98
  Chester - 65   Pheba - 1, 41
  Joe - 106   Robt. - 65
  John - 53   Vernen - 83
  Lewis/Louis - 1, 41,
     65, 83
ABNEY
  Martha - 38   Miles - 83
ABSHEAR
  Arthur - 83
ADAMS
  Mary - 1   Randall - 1
  Nannie/Nanie - 1, 99
ADDISON
  Isaac - 105   Josie - 105
AKERS
  Alice - 1   Perdelia - 48
  Amon - 84   Rhoda - 1*
  Cath. - 23, 101   Stephen - 1*
  Evaline - 24   Wm. - 48
  Laura - 1
ALDER
  Harvey - 1   Wm. - 1
  Susan - 1
ALDRIDGE
  Jessie - 97
ALEXANDER
  C. H. - 84

ALLEN
    Harris - 84
    Kittie - 104
AMBURGH[Y]/AMBERGA
    Cath. - 72*
    Letta - 51
ANDERSON
    Lene - 88
ANGEL/ANGELL
    Amos - 1
    Andrew - 41*
    Eliz. - 11
    Ephraim - 53
    Henderson - 1
    James - 41
    Julius - 53
    Malvin - 41*
    Marinda - 63
ARNOLD/ARNEL
    Arminta - 2*
    Darsie - 65
    Eliza - 109
    G. W. - 75
    Geo. W. - 2*, 53
    Harriet - 23
    Isabell - 14
    J. C. - 84
    James - 2*
    John - 84
    Joseph - 84
    L. D. - 65, 75*, 84
    Lorenzo D. - 2, 53
    Lucy - 2
    Lula - 99
    Lydia - 2
ARROWOOD
    Jesse - 2
ASBELL/ASBILL
    Eliza   - 53
    Henry - 53
    Martitia - 44
    Mary - 2
ASBERRY/ASBERY
    John - 2
    Lou E. - 67

W. B. - 84
Wm. - 84

Lucinda - 51
Robt. - 51

Mary - 93
Merilda - 1
Rebeca - 1
Susan - 53
Vinnia - 63
W. J. - 84
Wilburn - 1, 63
Wm. - 1
Zerilda - 1

Mandy - 5
Mannie - 69
Mary/Polly - 2*,
    53, 75*
Minie - 2
N. J. - 109
Newton - 2
Phillip - 2
Rosa - 92
Rutherford - 75
Sarah/Sallie - 2*,
    63
Susan - 62
Udocia - 38
Wm. - 2
Zachary - 2

Sarah - 2

Paulina/Polina -
    8*, 43
Robt. - 2
Samuel - 2, 53

Nancy - 2
Wm. - 2

116

ASHCRAFT
    Algernon - 2, 41   Martha - 65
    Brutis - 65   Mary J. - 2
    Damen(?) - 65   Minnie - 2
    Dillard - 75   Nancy - 27, 33, 75
    Eliz. - 53   Ollie - 94
    Frank - 84   Rachel - 52
    Gideon/Gillard - 75*   Ruth - 2
    Hannah - 2*, 41   Sarah/Sally -
    James - 53   61, 73
    John - 2, 84   Wm. - 2*, 41, 53

BACK
    Wm. - 85
BAILEY/BALEY
    Ada - 87   Jennie(?) - 75
    Charley - 85   Malinda - 58
    Everet - 85   Mary - 75
    G. A. - 85   Richard - 75
BAKER (see also BARKER)
    Clarinda - 49, 60   Margaret - 41
    D. - 95   Mary - 41
    Evaline/Eveline/   Oscar - 85
       Evoline - 31*, 32   Wm. - 85
    John - 41
BALDWIN
    male - 3   Wm. - 3
    Celia - 3
BALL
    Ella - 85
BANKS
    Moses - 85   Rosa - 103
BANNER
    Polly - 5
BANNET/BANNETT (see also BENNETT & BARNETT)
    A. J. - 90   Alice - 90
BARKER
    Cornealus - 65   Sabina - 3
    John - 3*   Sarah - 65
    Joseph - 65   Sifa - 3
    Mary - 1, 3   Wm. - 85
    Rachel - 3
BARNETT
    Lucy - 23*

BARRETT
    -----? (fem) - 65
    Annie - 101
    Clarinda - 3
    Eliza - 41
    Eliz. - 41
    Fannie - 65*, 75
    Florence - 99
    G. B. - 85
    Harges - 75
    Harrison/Harison -
      3, 42
    Isom - 41
    Jack - 101
    James - 42, 57, 65
    Jane - 87
    Jesse - 85
BARRUS(?)
    Annie - 106
BARTLETT/BARTLETTE
    Emery - 104
BATES
    Clara - 106
BEACH
    Clifton - 3, 42, 54
    Katie - 113
    Lizzie/Lizza - 3, 42
BEAN
    Burrell - 85
BEATTY
    Anna - 18
    Baxter - 3
    Caroline/Carline -
      3, 42
    Edmond - 3
    Fanny/Fannie - 3*
    Harriet A. - 59
BEGLEY
    blank - 3
    Adaline - 42
    Allen - 75
    Bradley - 75
    Caly - 3
    Elisha H. - 4
    Floyd - 86
    G. D. - 3
    Geo. - 42

John - 42, 65*, 75*
Joseph - 65
Jossie - 65
Levisa/Louisa - 42
Matilda - 42, 57
Mattison - 75
Mary - 68, 78
Nannie - 91
Rachel - 75
Rebecca/Rebeca -
  42, 57
Rosa Ann - 3, 42
Varrison - 3
Vicy/Visa - 3*
Wm. - 100

Laura - 70

John - 106

Mary - 3
Samuel - 42

James - 3*, 42
Jane - 30
Lena - 3
Milo - 3, 86
Rhoda - 56
Richard - 86
Thos. - 54

H. P. - 86
Hettie - 4
Hiram - 66
James - 42
John - 3, 4
Kammon - 86
Margaret - 4
Martin - 42
  (cont.)

BEGLEY (cont.)
    Mary - 3, 4, 42
    Nancy Ann - 87
    Rachel - 3
    Sinda - 66
BELCHER
    Anna - 4
    Eliz. - 4
BELLAMY/BELOMY
    Cath. - 4
    Sarah - 4, 54
BELLMAN
    Emily - 102
BENNETT
    female - 4*
    male - 4
    Agnes - 4*
    Allie - 100
    Anna - 59
    Belinda - 4
BENTON
    Jesse - 86
BERGER/BURGER
    Augusta/Augusty - 19, 58
BESS
    Geo. W. - 4
    John - 4
BISHOP
    Ursula - 55
BLACKWELL
    Earnest - 86
BLEVINS
    Lillie - 104
BLOUNT
    Mildred/Millard -
        24, 25*
BOAZ
    Amanda - 105
BOOTH/BOOTHE/BOUTH
    Claude - 86
    Geo. W. - 54, 66
    John - 54, 66
BOWLES
    Amanda - 105
BOWLING/BOWLIN/BOLAN
    Callie - 4
    Keen/Kenis - 54, 86

Sis - 75
Swinfield/Swempfield
    - 4, 42
Walter - 66

Manson - 4
Wesley - 86

Wm. - 4

Isabella/Esbella - 4
John - 4*
Nancy - 4
Richard - 4*
Susan/Susannah - 4*
Wm. - 4

Lucinda - 59

Kizah - 4

Joanah - 57

Narcissa - 61
Rebecca - 54

Laura Jane - 66
Nancy - 54

Sarah - 4
Wm. - 4

BOWMAN(?)
   Major L. - 85
BOWMAN
   Alexander - 4
   Andrew J. - 5
   Anna - 5
   Arminta - 5
   Barney - 86
   Bedford - 86
   Bert - 94
   Callie - 66
   Dan - 87
   Dora - 103
   Elisha - 87
   Eliz. - 4, 5*, 29
   Fannie - 65*
   Fenton - 66

   Geniva - 15
   Green - 4
   Hulda - 103
   John - 5
   Lucy/Lizzie - 5
   Maranda/Miranda 28*
   Marium/Mariam - 7
   Matt - 66
   Nancy - 5
   Samuel - 66
   Sarah - 66, 110
   W. H. - 66
   Wesley/Weslie - 5*
   Zerilda - 20

BOYD
   Peter - 5
   Polly - 5

   Samuel - 5

BRANDENBURGH
   male - 5
   Alice - 66, 76
   Almeda - 5
   Amelia - 5
   Andrew - 5
   Annie - 70
   Arch - 87
   Asa - 66
   Brownlow - 87
   Burtie - 66
   C. C. - 66
   Callie - 102
   Cant - 87
   Carrie - 76
   Cath. - 5
   Chas. - 87
   Cleopatra - 98
   Cora - 87
   D. - 76, 87
   Daniel G. - 5
   David - 76, 87
   Debora - 54
   Delina - 30, 31
   Edna - 106
   Efford - 66
   Eliz. - 5

   Emeline - 66
   Eveline - 6, 70
   Ezra - 66
   Florence - 95
   Floyd - 87
   Geo. - 6
   Hardin - 5
   Houstin - 110
   Ida - 110
   Isham - 66
   Jackson - 5
   James - 5*, 66, 87
   Jerry - 87
   Joel - 5
   John/Jno. - 5*, 54,
      55, 66
   Jos. - 45
   Kenez - 5
   Lewis - 66
   Lillie - 101
   Logan - 76
   Louisa - 66, 76
   Lucy - 5, 6, 29, 53
   Malvry - 66
   Mandy - 5
      (cont.)

BRANDENBURGH (cont.)
   Margaret/Margret -
      5, 6
   Marie - 66
   Martha/Patsy - 5,
      42, 55, 66*
   Mary - 5*, 6,, 55
   Maryania - 66
   Mat - 66
   Matild[a] - 45
   Mattie - 66
   Morgan - 87
   N. - 76
   Nancy/Nannie - 5, 23,
      45, 55, 66, 76

R. R. - 87
Robt. - 87
Samuel - 5, 6, 54
Sarah - 5, 76
Shelby - 88
Simmie - 66
Simpson - 88
Sophia - 32
Susan - 11
T. - 76
T. Q(?) - 88
Thos. - 5, 88
Wm. - 5*

BRANS
   Viney -104

BRANSEN
   Eliza - 97

W. H. - 97

BREWER
   Eliz. - 62

Judah - 61

BRISCOE
   Frances - 37
   Kitty - 63
   Mary Frances - 37, 63

Wm. - 63

BRISK
   Cain - 88

BRITTON
   C. L. - 97

BROOKS
   Kittie - 89

BROWN
   James - 6, 54
   Lourena - 6

Susan - 6
Wilson - 88

BRYANT
   Anna - 6
   James - 6
   Martisha - 12
   Matilda - 12

Sabina - 3
Sena Lena - 6
Sifa - 3

BRYCRAFT(?)
   Vaughn - 88

BUCKHEART/BUCKHART
   Eliza - 14

Nancy - 20*

BUMGARDNER
   Margaret - 34

BURCHEM
   James - 6   Martha - 6
   Levisa - 6
BURGER (see BERGER)
BURKE/BURK
   Chas. - 88   John - 66
   Connie - 112   Maston - 88
   Droisa(?) - 96   Nannie - 66
   Effa - 6   Roxsie - 92
   Emmie(?) - 66   Vivia - 6
   Geo. - 6, 54
BURKHART
   Eliz. - 6   Nancy - 6
   Isaac - 6
BURNS/BURNES(?)
   Lucinda - 14, 57
BURNS
   Brice - 88   Merida - 88
   Martha - 72   Nancy - 30*
BURTON/BURTEN
   Agnes - 4*   Susan - 4
   J. J. - 88
BUSH
   Margaret - 18, 46   Tandy M. (see
   Rebecca - 30   Margaret)
BUTLER
   David - 89   John - 89
   Edgar - 66   Nancy - 66
   Jackson - 66

CABLE
   Carlton - 67, 76   Lucinda - 99
   Caroline (see Cynthia) Millard - 6
   Casper - 67, 76   Rebecca - 60
   Cynthia - 35   Sarah - 6
   Emily - 21, 22*   Thos. - 89
   Ettoffa - 6   Whig - 99
   Frances - 67, 76*
CALAHAN
   Lillian - 96
CALDWELL
   Eliz. - 54   Jonas - 89
   Freeland - 54   Wm. - 54
CALIMES/CALMES
   Sarah - 24   Wm. - 89
CAMASK(?)
   Henry - 89

CAMASK/CAMACK
    -----? (fem) - 72   Lillie - 94
    Albert - 89   Martha - 67
CAMPBELL/CAMBELL
    Eva - 93   Sam - 89
CARROLL
    C. C. - 89   Keneth - 89
CARSON
    Robt. - 90
CARTER
    Andy - 93   Mattie - 95
CARTRIGHT
    Napoleon - 90
CASITY
    David - 6   Mary - 6
    Edmond - 6
CENTERS
    America - 6   Rachel - 6
    Maggie - 73   Stephen - 6
CHAMBERS
    John - 7   Mary - 15
    Joseph - 7   Rebecca - 42
    Lydia Ann - 57   Robt. - 42
    Malvina/Malvan/Malvar   Sarah - 35*, 51
      - 27, 49*   Weeden - 90
    Marium/Mariam - 7   Wm. - 42
CHAPMAN
    Sarah - 73
CHARLES
    Frank - 55   Mart - 113
CHILDERS
    Chas. - 67   Lucinda - 67
    Curt - 90   Mary - 42
    Jane - 42   Rosa - 73
    Lloyd - 67   W. H. - 42
CHILSON
    Albert - 7   Margaret/Margret -
    Lucy - 7   7
CHRISMAN
    Nancy - 60
CLARK
    Annie - 82   Henry - 82
    Barthena - 82   James - 90

CLAY
   Bell - 7   John - 7
   Henry - 7
CLUTCH
   Lizzie - 90
CLUTS(?)
   Mattie - 95
CO-----?
   Mary - 76
COCKERHAM/COCKRAN
   Chester - 65   Margaret - 7*
   Dora - 7   Martin - 7*
   Gilly Ann - 21, 59   Orlena - 7
   Emily - 59   Sarah - 55
   James - 55, 59   Zachariah - 7
   Lydia/Lydda - 7*   Zachary Taylor - 55
COCKRELL/COCKERELL
   Emily - 103   Mary - 19
COCKRUM/CONUN(?)
   Sally/Sallie - 34, 35
COFFER
   Nancy - 2
COLE
   Alice - 66   Martitia - 12
   Amanda - 80   Mary/Polly - 35, 76
   America - 7*   Medly - 67
   Annie - 80   Minnie - 67
   Armina - 7   Nancy/Nannie - 7*
   Austin/Ostin - 42*   Nettie - 7
   Bessie - 86   Paulina - 20, 42
   Birdine - 7   Price - 103
   Chas. - 7   Rhoda - 43*
   Fannie - 67   Robert - 7, 90
   Felix - 7, 80   Rosie - 69
   James - 89   Speed - 7*
   John - 29, 67   Stanley - 90
   Lena - 103   Susan - 43
   Logan - 90   T. (fem) - 76
   Lucy Jane - 111   Thos. - 43
   Martha - 89, 102   Wm. - 7, 55, 76
   Martha Ellen - 55   Zilla - 7
COLLINS
   male - 7   Polly Ann - 8
   Howard - 7, 8, 90   Wm. - 89
   Nancy - 7, 8
COLLY
   H. H. - 90

COMBS
   Amanda - 82
   Armina/Arminia -
      76, 102
   Bertha - 90
   Christina/Christenia
      - 21*
   Cordelia - 107
   Dillas - 90
   Dora - 104
   Elbert - 91
   Eliza - 8
   Farinda - 28
   Georgia - 102
   Gertrude - 95
   Henry - 90
   Ida - 67, 76
   J. G. - 91
   James - 91
   John - 91
   Joseph - 8
   Kenneth - 8
COMEALISON
   Cora - 73
   Ida - 80
CONGLETON
   Ada - 8, 43
   Isaac - 8*, 43
   Lilly - 8
CONKWRIGHT
   Ada - 113
COOMER
   male - 8
   Abb - 91
   Andy - 91
   Benj./Ben - 8, 110
   Callie - 66
   Crittenden - 43
   Daisey - 103
   David - 8, 43
   Eleanor - 8
   Eliz. - 8*
   Emeline - 8
   Henry - 8*
   Jackson - 9
   James - 8, 43
   Jesse - 8, 43

Lucy - 94
M. (fem) - 82
Malissa - 9
Margaret/Margret -
   8, 30*
Mary - 8
Minnie - 85
Mulary - 93
Ned - 76
Ollie - 109
Oscar - 91
Otto - 67
Pely - 8
S. L. - 91
Sarah - 8*, 67
Tinsley - 8*
Varina - 28
Walter - 91
Wm. - 67, 82
Williamette - 8

Polly Ann - 80
Wm. - 80

Mahelia - 96
Myrtie - 105
Paulina - 8*, 43

Melvin - 91

Leander - 8
Logan - 91
Louisa - 9
Lourana - 8
Martha - 8, 43
Mary - 8
Nancy/Nannie/Nanna
   - 8*, 43
Patton - 8
Riley - 8, 55
Sarah/Sally - 8,
   55, 93
Susan M. - 9
T. - 55
   (cont.)

COOMER (cont.)
    Taylor/Tyler - 8, 43   Vina - 28
    Tom - 91
COOPER
    Alfred - 55   Thos. - 91
    Rachel/Racheal - 37*, 38*
CORNELIUS
    Susan - 1
CORNETT
    Allice - 91   Flora - 69
    Amanda - 76*   Jane - 43, 50
    Brand - 76   John - 29
    Cely - 52   Martha - 43, 50, 76
    Ednie - 108   Mary - 76
    Eli - 43, 50   P. C. - 76
    Eva - 76
CORUM
    Daniel - 43   Wm. - 43
    Paulina - 43
COTTONGIM
    Minerva - 64
COUCH/CROUCH
    Albert - 92*   Leah - 81
    Amanda - 92   Maggie - 102
    America - 12   Margaret - 25, 76
    Anna - 9*   Martha - 67
    Barny - 9   Mary - 67
    Buch - 81   Minnie - 67
    Daisy - 67   Nancy - 43
    Eli - 55   Patience/Patient -
    Elijah - 43   67
    Enoch - 35   Rane - 81
    Fannnie - 55   Rose - 73
    Farmer - 67   Simp - 92*
    Geo. - 92   Ursula - 55
    Henry - 9*   Vicy/Visa - 3*
    James/Jim - 92*   Wm. - 67
    John - 43
COX
    Lucy - 72

CRABTREE
David - 9
Eliza - 9, 43
Eliz. - 9*
Elkana - 9
Geo. - 9, 43
Horace - 9
Ida - 67, 76
Jacob - 43
James - 67
Job - 43
CRAWFORD
America - 9*, 44
Armilda - 9
Avary - 18
Cally - 9
Cynthia Ann - 9
Daniel Boone - 9
Dilla - 9, 44
Elihu - 9
Eliz./Lizzie -
    3, 9, 54
Emily - 44
Geo. W. - 9
Hanah - 9
CREECH
C. - 93
Dewitt - 9
Dora - 99
Earl - 67
Elijah - 55
Floyd - 9, 67
Henry - 55
J. D. - 67
Jessie - 86
Lou E. - 67
CRITZER
Almeda - 10
Almelia - 10
Idama - 10
CROACH/CROOCK(?)
Nancy - 10
Nancy Ann - 10

L. (fem) - 81
L. K. - 81
Levisa/Louisa - 42
Lou - 81
Malissa - 9
Manerva - 67
Mary - 9
Rebecca - 43
Rosa - 43

James - 9*, 44*
Jerry - 92
Letha/Litha - 9, 44
Marcus - 9, 44
Mary/Polly - 18,
    111
Nancy - 7, 24
Nancy Bell - 9
O. - 55
Susan/Susannah - 9,
    44, 48
Sylvana - 34
Wm./Bill - 44, 90

Lula - 67
Lydie - 110
Malvry - 66
Margret - 71
Martha - 77*
Matilda - 9
Myrtle - 67
Nancy - 55
Robt. - 92
Stephen - 92

Leander - 10*
Margaret - 10

Sylvester - 10

CROOK
    Cath. - 10*
    Chas. - 10, 67*, 77
    Enos - 67
    Logan - 67, 77
CUNDIFF
    Laura - 91
    Mary - 10
CURRY
    Amanda/Amandy - 68,
        77*
    Andrew - 44
    Chas. - 77
    Eliza - 10*
    Ellen - 44, 77
    Geo. - 10*
    George E. - 10
    Hargis/Hargnes - 68,
        77

    Mathew - 10*
    Maud - 67*, 77
    Wm. - 10, 92

    Nancy - 10
    Robt. - 10, 92

    James - 10*, 77*
    John - 68, 77
    Louvina - 10*
    Luviny(?) - 77
    Margaret - 10
    Nancy - 60
    Ollie - 86
    Sarah - 68
    Wm. - 44

DAMRELL/DAMERIL/DAMERAL/DAMERALL
    Eliz. - 10, 11
    Fannie - 108
    Franklin - 55
    Joel - 10, 11, 44
    John - 11
    Josephine - 11
    Laron - 92
    Lucinda - 11
DANEL/DANELL (DANIEL?)
    Corela - 100
DANIEL
    Albert F. - 11
    Alfred - 11
    Matilda - 11
DAVIDSON
    Margaret - 4
    Mary - 4, 42
    Maud - 91
DAVIES
    Roderick - 56
DAVIS
    male - 11
    Andy - 93
    Annie - 70
    Cath. - 24
    Demaris/Demmy - 11

    Lucy - 68
    Margrett - 109
    Minnie - 96
    Phoebe/Pheba - 10,
        11, 44*
    Sally - 55
    Samuel - 55

    W. C. - 100

    Scott - 11
    Susan - 11
    Wm. - 11

    Nancy - 109
    Rachel - 3

    Florence/Flawrence
        - 73
    Geo. - 93
        (cont.)

128

DAVIS (cont.)
    George Ann/Georgiann   Leler - 83
        - 11*, 44   Maud - 113
    James - 11*, 44   Nannie - 11
    Julia - 11   Orlando - 11
DAY
    Diana - 11   Mary - 5
    Eliza - 11   Newbery - 11
    Green B. - 11   Walter - 93
    Ira - 11   Willie - 11
DEATON/DEATEN
    Alfred - 11, 12, 56   Maggie - 84
    Alwilda - 11   Marsie(?) - 95
    Armina - 77   Martha - 77
    Callie - 92   Mary/Polly - 11
    Cath. - 92   Nancy - 93*, 105
    Dison - 11   Price - 93
    Fanny - 11   Rebecca - 12, 56
    George - 11   Sarah - 12, 92, 93,
    Grant - 77   105
    Green - 92, 93   Sheldon - 93
    Hettie - 93   Wm. Price
    James - 12   (see Price)
    John - 12, 56, 93*, 105
DEERING
    Thos. - 93
DENNIS
    Boone - 93   J. P. - 68
    C---? C---- - 68   Sarah - 68
DICKERSON
    Cordelia - 108   James - 44, 56
    Edw. - 44   Jno. - 56
    Emily - 44   Matilda - 56
DITMAN
    Jesse - 12   Sallie - 12
    Polly - 12
DIXON
    Louisa/Loula/Lucella/Luella - 39*, 40*, 52
    Mattie - 24
DOUGHERTY
    Francis - 12   Mallie - 44
    Frank - 44   Martitia - 12, 44
    Henry - 12
DUFF
    George Ann/Georgiann   Lenord - 93
        - 11*   Matilda - 44
    James - 44

DUGGER
    Sarah - 65
DUKE
    Joseph - 56
DUNAGAN/DUNAGIN/DUNIGAN
    Alice - 84
    Amanda - 12*
    America - 12
    Berry - 12*, 93
    Chas. - 12
    Clara - 77
    Edna - 77
    Eliz. - 12, 44, 56
    F. (fem) - 77*
    Grant - 93
    Harlin - 93
DUNAWAY
    Benj. - 44
    Charley - 12
    Clide - 77
    David - 44, 94
    Elis - 92
    Eliz. - 12, 44, 45,
        56
    John - 45, 56, 77
    Lucinda - 104
    Margaret - 98, 108
DURBIN
    -----? (fem) - 68
    ---lie(?) (fem) - 68
    Ambrose - 13
    Demia - 13
    Edward - 13
    Eliz. - 13, 33
    Emeline - 13
    Evoline - 13
    Hade - 112
    J. M. - 94
    James - 94
    John - 13, 45, 56
    Joseph - 13, 45, 56
    Josiah - 13
    Julia - 27
    Lucian - 94
    Lucinda - 56
    Lucyan - 13

Levisa - 64

Isaac - 44
J. E. - 104
James - 12*
Jula - 99
L. - 77*
Martisha - 12
Matilda - 12
Nancy - 7, 8, 12,
    44
Wm. - 12
Zura(?) - 12

Mazilla - 12
Pauline - 45
Priscilla - 44
Quintilla - 12*,
    13, 45
Sarah - 77
Spicy - 44
Thos. - 12*, 44, 56
Wm./Willie - 12*,
    13*, 45*, 94

Luster - 94
Malinda - 13
Marion - 13*
Mary - 13, 112
Mary Ann - 45
Minna/Minnia - 13,
    63
Nancy - 19, 45
Rebecca - 13
Ruth - 98
Sally - 45
Serra(?) - 97
Surilla - 56
Walter(?) - 68
Wm. - 13*, 45
Zeraney - 105
Zerilda - 45

EAGER(?)
-----? (fem) -68   Wm. Thos. - 68
P. T. - 68
EDENS
Amanda - 13   John - 13*
EDITINGTON/ELINGTON
Bean - 77   Eliza - 77
Ed - 77
EDWARDS
Lewellen - 88   John - 94
ELINGTON (see EDITINGTON)
ELLIOTT
Dawson - 56
ENGLISH
Wm. - 94
ESTEP
Nancy - 30
ESTES
male - 13   Laura/Laurinda - 56
Amanda - 37   86, 94
Anna Belle - 86   Maggie - 94
Anthony - 94   Margaret - 14
Asberry - 13   Martha/Mashel -
Clarinda - 13   13*, 14
Ellen - 94   Mary/Polly - 12,
Emily - 13   14, 29
Emily Jane - 56*   Mason - 13*, 14
Fielding - 56*, 62   Nancy - 14
Henry - 14, 56   Nannie(?) - 96
Hiram - 14   Quintilla - 12*, 45
Ibby/Abba - 13   Sarah - 14, 36*
Jacob - 14   Sarah Ann - 62
Joan/Joannah - 60   Wm. - 56, 86, 94
EVANS
male - 14   Jesse - 14, 57, 78
Clay - 68   Lucy - 68
Edaom - 78   Martha - 14, 110
Eliz. - 14   Mary/Polly - 57
Emma - 73   Nancy/Nannie - 5,
Hiram - 57   68
Huram - 14   Nettie - 112
Isabell - 14   Sinda - 66
EVE
Anna - 14   Wm. - 14
Sally - 14
EWING(?)
Wm. - 98

131

FAIRCHILDS
    Lucy - 2
FARGOT
    Alex. - 94
FARLER
    John - 14   Mary - 14
    Martha - 14
FARLEY
    Mattie Lee - 98
FARMER
    Bertie - 95   Martha - 54
    Caroline - 32   Matild[a] - 45
    Clarkie - 87   Mattie - 107
    Dewey - 68   Nancy - 21
    Eliza - 8   Perdillia - 68
    John - 14, 68   Sidney - 94
    Lena - 94   Silas - 14
    Lillie - 102   Simpson - 57
    Margaret - 14
FAULKNER
    Geo. - 57   Polina - 113
FIELDS
    Benj. F. - 14   Josephine - 14
    David - 14   Lona - 45
    E. C. - 94   Mary/Polly - 14
    Emily - 107   Minerva - 61
    Harrison - 14   Nancy - 61
    Hiram - 14   W. H. H. - 45
    John - 94
FIKE
    Elihue - 68, 78   Lee/Leander - 14
    Fred - 68   Lucinda - 14
    George A. - 112   Mary - 68, 78
    Joseph - 14, 57   Stanley - 78
FLANNERY/FLANERY
    Cath. - 10*   Pearl - 68
    Eliz. - 45*   Rachel - 45
    James - 68   Spencer - 45*
    Kate - 85   Wm. H. - 45
    Nannie - 68
FLETCHER
    Eliza - 14   Nancy - 6
    Levisa - 6   Shelba - 14
    Merida - 14   Violet - 15*
FLINCHUM
    Charley - 95   Rebecca Jane - 95
    J. B. - 95

FORTNER
   Geo. - 57
FOURBIN
   Alley May - 113
FOUTS
   Henry - 95
FOWLER
   Caroline - 32   Letha/Litha - 9, 44
FOX
   Adie - 90   Nancy Belle - 89
   Alice - 91   Sarah/Sally - 78,
   John - 78   92
   Louzy - 98   Thos. - 78
FRAILEY/FRALEY
   female - 15   John - 95*
   B. Delli - 15   Lou Ellen - 15
   Benj. - 15   Lucinda - 15
   Butler D. - 15   Stephen - 15*
   Helen - 15   Susan - 15*
   Henry - 15*   Violet - 15*
   James - 15*
FRANCE
   Alba - 34   Helen - 15
   Cath. - 4   Josephine - 15
   Geniva - 15   Lewis - 15
FRAZIER
   Almelia - 10
FREEMAN
   Gerty - 97   Martha - 27
FREY (see also FRYE)
   Eliz. - 45
FRISBEY
   Ollie Belle - 104
FRYE (see also FREY)
   Rachel - 89
FULKS
   Henry - 15*   Nancy - 15*
   Juletta - 15   Wm. - 15

GABBARD/GABARD
   Claiborne - 15, 64   Martha - 66
   Delina - 69   Mary - 15, 39, 64,
   Dora - 69   74
   Geo. - 57   Minerva - 64
   John - 57   Ollie - 103
   Lillie - 97   Rachel - 15
   Logan - 95   Sarah - 66

GALE
   Lucy - 37
GARLAND
   Eliz. - 22   Prior - 57*
   Margaret - 57
GAY
   Nora - 96
GENTRY
   Diademia - 15   Mariam - 15
   Joseph - 15   Robt. - 95
GERLEY (see GOURLEY)
GIBS
   John - 113   Lizzie - 113
GILBERT
   Coleman - 95   Maryania - 66
   Eliz. - 16   Michle (Michael?) -
   Francis - 46   46
   Herbert - 78   Phoeba - 46
   John - 16, 78   Sally - 46
   Letcher - 46   Thos. - 78*
   Martha - 16   Wm. - 46
   Mary - 78*
GILLESPIE/GILESPEE
   Eiz. - 5   Susan - 16
   Hiram - 16   Wm. - 16
GILLUM/GILUM
   Annabell - 46   Sarah - 46
   Marion - 46
GIPSON
   Oma - 68
GODFREY
   John - 68   Oma - 68
   Nancy - 68
GOE
   Arthur - 16   Phillip - 16
   Benj. - 16*   Robt. - 68
   Mary - 16*   W. B. - 68
   Netie(?) - 74   Willie - 68
GOFORTH
   Henry - 95
GOOD
   Richard - 95
GOODWIN
   Laura Jane - 66

GOOSEY
   Armina - 16   Manda - 16
   David - 16*   Maryann - 70
   Josephine - 16*   Sarah - 8*
GORDON/GORDEN
   Eliz. - 14   Susanah - 36, 58
   Lucy - 32, 51
GOURLEY/GERLEY
   Hanah - 16   Lucinda - 53
   J. C. - 53   Mary - 2, 53
   John - 16   Walter - 16
GRANT
   Edda (male) - 95
GRAY
   Benj. - 46   Lucy- 16
   Ellen - 16   Luvina - 22
   H. K. - 69   Margaret - 14
   Harden - 16   Mary - 16*
   Hulbert - 69   Nestie - 69
   John - 16   Robt. - 16
   Lillie - 108   Wm. - 16*, 108*
GREER/GREEN(?)
   Frances - 78   Jesse - 78
   I. J. (fem) - 78
GRIFFIN
   Ara - 16   Jesse - 16
   Benj. - 16   Mary - 16, 17
   Bitha - 16   Rosanna - 17
   Chas. - 16, 17
GROSS
   Clifton - 96   Malvin - 41*
   Eliza - 41   Minnie - 94
   Henry - 41   Ned - 78
   Julia - 78   Robt. - 96
   Leanna - 98   Sam - 96
   Louis - 96   Wm. - 78
   Louisa - 41
GUM
   Amelia Ann - 1, 41   Lucinda - 23*, 59
   Cath/Kitsey - 17   Mary - 33, 46
   Edy - 33   Nancy - 46
   Eliz. - 17   Narcissa Jane - 59
   Ella - 33   Stephen - 17
   Greenberry - 46   Susan - 15
   Lou Ellen/Lew Ellen   W. B. - 59
      - 15, 25

135

HADDIX
    Charley - 96
HALE
    James - 17
    Mary Jane - 17
HALEY
    Abba - 17
    Austin - 17*, 57
    Frank - 17
HALL
    -----? (fem) - 69
    Amanda - 70
    Brownlow - 96
    Callie - 78
    Carlos - 69
    Charlie - 69
    Cordelia - 17
    Eliz. - 57
    Fannie - 69
    Geo. - 96
    H. H. - 78
    Harvey/Harvey Jr.
        - 17, 46, 78
HAMILTON/HAMELTON
    B. J. - 96
    Chas/Charley - 69, 96
    Dora - 100
    Elmer - 69
    John - 17
    Kate - 101
    Liza - 69
HAMMAN
    B. F. - 78
    Eliz. - 17, 18
    James - 58
    John - 17, 18
    Oma - 17
    Phebe - 18
HAMPTON
    Avary - 18
    Chaney - 19*, 46
    Clarsa - 19
    Jefferson - 9, 18
    Laura - 98
    Lucy - 18

Ruben - 57

Nancy - 46
Wm/Wm. Jr - 17, 46*

James - 57
Mary - 17*
Nannie - 57

Henry - 78
John - 17*, 58
Joseph - 17*
Kate - 106
Leslie - 78
Lucy Ann - 17*
Mannie - 69
Mary - 17*, 55, 78,
    86
Permelia - 17, 46
Sarah - 17, 46
Wm. - 69

Lucy - 17
Malinda - 13
Martha - 17
Mollie - 69
Rhoda - 27
Willard - 69
Wm. - 69

Phillip/Philip -
    18, 31, 58
Robt. - 18
Sindar - 78
Susan - 58
Thos. - 18, 78

Malissa - 18
Martha - 18
Mary - 18
Samuel - 18
Violet - 18
Wilson - 18

HANDY
   Eliz. - 72
HANN
   O. A. - 96
HARPER
   Carl - 96
HARRIS
   John - 18   Wm. - 18
   Maggie - 18
HARRISON
   A. J. - 97
HATTON
   Armina - 18   Mary - 18
   Ben - 97   R. R. - 97
   Eliza - 18   Wm. - 18*
   Jane - 18
HAYES/HAYS/HAYSE
   Chas. - 97   Margret - 25
   Evaline - 72   Mary - 71
   Lurana - 25   Ursula Jane - 103
HENSLEY
   Hester Jane - 61   Polly - 11
HERALD
   Violet - 18
HERENDON
   -----? (fem) - 69
HIERONYMOUS
   Cordy - 18   Tandy M. (see
   Geo. - 46   Margaret)
   Margaret - 18, 46   Thomas - 18, 46
HILL
   Abba - 18   Mary - 19, 37
   Anna - 18   Pallo Allo - 18
   Arrena - 18*   Robt. - 19
   James - 18   Samuel - 18
   John - 18*   Wm. - 19
   Kenlee - 97
HOBBS
   C. B. - 97   Margaret - 33*
   Cath. - 51   Mary Ann - 19
   Cora - 19   Sarah - 19*, 46
   Eliza - 39   Senda(?) - 6
   Hugh - 97   Wm. - 19*, 46
   Isaac - 46

HOGAN
    Armilda - 84   J. J. - 97
    Ella - 96   Jim - 84
    Fanny - 84   Lou Ellen - 93
    Hallie - 88   W. A. - 97
    Harrison - 88
HOLBROOK
    Tempa - 46
HOLLAND
    Archd. - 19   Ellen - 69
    Chaney - 19*, 46   Flem - 69
    Clarsa - 19   Malissa - 19
    Edward - 69   Tarlton - 19*, 46
    Eliz. - 29
HOLLINGSWORTH
    Crittenden - 43   Martha - 43
HOOTON(?)
    Maud - 96
HOOVER
    Lucy - 6   Provie - 88
    Mary Jane - 17
HORN(?)
    Aaron - 82   Rebecca - 82
    Elihue(?) - 82
HORN
    -----? (fem) - 78   Rebecca - 38*
    -----? (male) - 78*   Sarah - 86
    Aaron/Aron - 47, 90   Sidey - 19
    Duglas - 97   Suzan - 47
    John - 19   Wilburn - 97
    Kate - 90   Wm. - 58
    Manda - 47
    Nancy/Nancy Ann - 10, 19
HOUNSHELL
    Frank - 47   Milly - 47
    Judah- 47
HOUSTON/HUSTON
    Ellen - 95   May - 71
HOWARD
    Clem - 45   Samuel - 58
    Mary/Mary Ann -   Sarilda/Zerilda -
       16*, 45   32*
    Nancy - 45

HOWELL
   Alice - 108   Mary - 14, 19
   Decatur - 19   Mattie - 69
   Elias - 19*   Mitchell - 98
   Eliza - 19, 47   Rebecca - 36*
   Eveline - 19   Rosie - 69
   John - 69   Samuel - 19, 47
   Layfayet - 98   Simpson - 19
   Leanah/Leonia - 19*   Thos. - 69
   Margaret Ann - 47   Wm. - 19
HOWERTON
   Albert - 19, 58   John - 19*
   Augusta - 19   Mary - 19
   Bell - 19   Nancy - 19
   Chas. - 19
HUGHES
   Chas. - 69   Mattie - 69
   Edward - 58   Sid - 69
   Kizah - 4
HUMES
   Cliff - 98
HUNTER
   Hester Jane - 61
HURLEY
   John/Jno. - 20, 47*   Mary - 47
   Mahaley- 20   Paulina - 20
HURST
   Norbin - 98

INGRAM
   Ara - 16   Margret - 70
   F. M. - 69   Mary - 17
   Flora - 69   Nannie - 88
   Gladis - 101   Nettie - 69
ISAACS
   Martha - 17   Rebecca - 30
   Mary - 83   W. P. - 98
ISOM
   Willie - 98

JACKSON
   Mariah - 87   Shelby - 98

JAMESON
    Eliz. - 29*
    Errilda Neva - 20
    John - 20
    Martha/Patsy - 35
    Mary Ann - 23
JETT
    Chas. - 98
JEWELL
    David - 20
    Lillie - 108
JOHNS
    Eunice - 62
JOHNSON
    female - 69
    Amelia - 47
    Anderson - 69
    Anna - 47
    Arrela/Orrelia -
      26, 49
    Celia - 3
    David - 47*
    Delina/Delara - 69
    Dora - 69
    Eliza - 53
    Eliz./Lizzie - 104
    Florence - 26, 60
    Henry - 69
    James - 79
    Jeff - 98, 108
    John - 58
    Jossie - 69
    Lilly/Lillie - 79, 84
    Lora - 69
    Lucinda - 20
JONES
    Breckenridge - 20
    Derias - 47
    Eliz. - 4
    Eunice/Unice Malissa
      - 47, 62
    Gilly Ann - 20
    Henry - 79*
    J. M. - 99
    John - 20*, 47, 99
    Joshua - 47
    Leslie - 99

    Patience/Patient -
      29, 67
    Rhoda - 1*
    Sarah - 20
    Sarilda - 20

    Jane - 98

    Lucinda - 20
    Wesley - 20

    Mary/Polly Ann -
      47*, 57, 58
    Minnie - 99
    Nancy/Nannie - 79,
      96
    Naoma - 20
    Patience - 67
    Robt. - 20
    S. - 79
    Sally/Sally Ann -
      20, 58, 71
    Samuel - 20
    Sopha - 79
    Thos. - 84
    Timothy - 20, 58
    Washington - 58
    Wilburn - 20
    Wm. - 79
    Zachary - 20
    Zerilda - 20*

    Llew Ellen - 20
    Mary/Mollie - 20,
      47, 79*, 102
    Nancy/Nannie - 20*,
      102
    Orca - 79
    Otta - 79
    Rebecca - 31, 61
    Rosa/Rosilla - 32,
      111
    Stephen - 20, 47

JUDD
  Biddy - 21, 47   Manda - 21
  James Rowland 21*, 47*   Martha - 21, 47
  Jane - 91   Nancy - 21*, 47*
  Lilly Ann - 21, 47   Rowland (see James)

KASH
  Lucinda - 58
KEENE
  Lydia - 7
KELLY/KELLEY
  -----? (fem) - 79   John - 21, 99
  -----? (male) - 79*   Margaret/Marget -
  Callie - 105   21, 48, 79
  Charlottie - 21   Speed - 21, 48
  Harun(?) - 99   Thomas - 21
  Henderson - 48   Wm. - 21
KENDRICK/KENDRICKS/KINDRICK
  Cynthia - 87   James - 58
  Eliz. - 113   Vista - 99
  H. - 87
KETCHAM
  Ellen - 40*   Jeremiah - 59
KEYWOOD
  Axie - 79   Mary - 79
  Henry - 79
KIDD
  David - 21   Lourana - 21
  Elijah - 21   Mariam - 21
  Elvira - 21, 48   Samuel - 21, 48
  John Samuel - 21   Wm. - 48
KILBURN
  Cath. - 21   Leslie - 99
  Christina/Christenia   Lourana/Lurania -
    - 21*   8, 55
  Florence - 88   Martin - 88
  Green - 103   Matilda - 55
  Greenberry - 21   Tipton - 21*
KINCAID
  -----? (fem) - 70   Dudley - 21
  Alice - 21   Edward - 21, 22*
  Ann - 76   Emily - 21, 22*
  Carrie - 70, 109   Frances - 67, 76*
  Chas. - 99   Geo. - 48*
  Cynthia/Cynthiann -   Gilly Ann - 21
    21, 59   Hettie - 70
  Douglas - 21, 99   (cont.)

141

KINCAID (cont.)
   Jacob - 99
   James - 59
   John - 22
   Linda - 89
   Luvina - 22
   Malissa - 22
   Margret/Peggy 48, 70
   Mariam - 15, 31*, 85
   Martha - 70
   Mary Ann - 31

   Melvin - 99
   Nancy - 59, 70
   Plummer - 21
   Robt. - 22
   Rutherford - 70
   Samuel Plummer - 59
   Socrates - 21, 59, 76
   Walter - 70

KINCANNON
   Mary J. - 29
KINDRICK (see KENDRICK)
KING
   male - 22
   Adison - 48
   Almilda/Alwilda -
      11, 12
   Alwilda - 22, 48*, 56
   Ann/Anna - 22*
   Atison - 22*
   Eliz. - 56
   Elvira - 21, 48
   Emiline - 22
   Green - 22

   Green Kelly - 22
   Jeremiah - 56
   John - 99
   Kelly (see Green)
   Lourana - 21
   Lydia/Lydda - 7*
   Melissa - 22
   Mollie - 69
   Sarah - 22
   Wm. - 22

KIRK
   female - 22
   Mahaley - 22

   Wm. - 22, 59

KOWLEN(?) (NOLEN?)
   Anderson - 99

LAMBERT
   A. S. - 100
LANDERS(?)
   Gilbert - 100
LANE
   James - 22
   John - 22

   Maggie - 110
   Orfa - 22

LAUTER(?)
   Elmer - 100
LAWSON/LOSSEN
   Armilda - 9
   Eliz. - 34
   J. B. - 100
   John - 100

   Maggie - 100
   Robt. - 100
   W. H. - 100
   Wm. - 100

LEGG
    Andrew - 59
    Hannah - 59
LEMASTER
    Bessie - 104
    Keen - 100
LETHGOE
    Luther - 101
LEWIS
    Sabra - 31
LIGHTFOOT
    Lucy - 54
LITTLE
    Evelyne - 93
LOCKARD
    Eliz. - 22
LONGSWORTH
    Geo. - 22
    Jane - 22
LUCAS
    female - 22
    Cyntha - 23
    Decorsey - 100
    Dona - 92
    E. E. - 70
    Elenor - 23
    Eliz. - 60
    Ellie - 109
    F. J. - 70
    Francis - 23
    Harriet - 23
    Harrison - 100
    Henry - 100
    James - 23, 48, 59
    Jesse - 23, 84
    Jno. - 109
LUDFORD
    Wm. - 101
LUTES
    male - 70
    Adda - 48
    Amanda - 70
    Andrew - 23
    Annie - 70*, 100
    Arch - 70
    C. C. - 70
    Chas. - 53, 59

James - 59
Roda - 108

Spence - 104

Nannie - 101

Wm. - 22*

Wm. - 22

Lillie - 70
Lucinda - 48
Lydia - 23
Mary Ann - 23
Mary Eliz. - 60
Nancy/Nannie/Nanna
    - 8, 43, 84
Pleasant - 23
Rachel - 113
Rebecca - 56
Robt. - 23
Samuel - 22
Sarah - 36
Tandy - 71
Wm. - 23*, 48, 59
Winnie - 22

Christopher - 48,
    59
Demia - 63
Dudley - 79
Ella - 110
Evoline - 79
F. M. - 70, 79
    (cont.)

LUTES (cont.)
    Fairlee - 70
    Frances - 70
    Francis - 59
    Georgia - 84
    Georgie - 65
    Horace -23
    J. N. - 70
    John - 23*
    Laura - 70
    Lena - 110
    Lot - 101
LYNCH
    Harvey - 23
    M. E. - 70
    Mary/Mary Ann - 16,
        70
    Nancy - 23
LYONS
    George A. - 23
    Hariet - 23

McCALL
    Pete - 101
McCLANCEY
    Lizzie - 88
McCLURE/McLURE
    Delitha - 37, 38
    James - 23*
McCULLUM
    Eliz. - 53
McDANIEL
    A. - 101
McGLOSON
    Liza - 69
McGUIER(?)
    Mary - 85
McGUIRE
    A. B. - 24
    Ansel - 48
    Archibald - 24*, 79
    Benj. - 48
    Callie - 106
    Caroline/Carline -
        3, 42
    Cath. - 23*, 24, 48,
        90, 101

Lucinda - 23*, 48,
    53, 59
Lurinda - 59
Mabel - 86
Mamy - 70
Margret - 7, 55
Nancy - 70
Samuel - 59
Sarah - 53
Simpson - 70

Perdillia - 68
Thos. - 23
Walter - 101
Wm. - 70

John - 107
Wm. - 23

Lucy - 23*
Samuel - 23

Sarah - 101

Chas. - 24
Demaris/Demmy/
    Didema/Diadema -
    11, 44, 48, 52
Eliza - 104
Eliz. - 17, 18
Ella - 31
Evaline - 24, 42
    (cont.)

144

McGUIRE (cont.)
    Felix - 24
    Frances - 28*
    Helen - 24*
    Henry - 101
    James - 42, 44, 101
    John Warwick - 48,
        101
    Joseph - 24
    Julia - 24
    Lin - 101
    Lucy - 24
    Margarett/Margret/
        Marget - 24, 79, 81
    Martha - 24
    Mary/Polly - 35*
    Mattie - 24
    Milton - 24
    Monroe - 24
    Rebecca - 54
    Susan - 36
    Thos. - 24, 79, 81
    Vivia - 6, 54
    Warwick (see also
        John Warwick) 23
    Wm. - 54
    Zerilda - 20
McINTIRE
    Mariam - 61
McINTOSH
    -----? (male) - 79*
    Anna - 103
    Chester -70
    Eveline - 70
    Larkin - 70
    Lennie - 79
    Lucy - 100
    Melviny(?) - 79*
    Robt. - 79
    S. - 87
    Thos. - 100
McKINNEY/McKINNIE/McKENEY
    -----? (fem) - 79
    Dillard(?) - 70
    Ellie(?) - 70
    James - 24
    Laura - 109
    Lucy - 70
    Samuel - 24, 101
    Sarah - 24
McLANE
    Elbert - 60
McQUEEN
    James - 24
    John - 24
    Nancy - 24
    Phebe - 24
    Samuel - 24
    Viola - 106
    Wm. - 24
McQUINN/McQUIN
    C. T. - 101
    J. F. - 101

MADEN
    Mary - 17
MADDOX/MADDIX/MADOX
    Bell - 7
    Lourena/Lourenia - 6, 54
    Martha - 57
    Mary - 17*, 57
MALAYER
    Mattie - 107

MALONEY
    Cora - 24
    Eliza - 18
    Eliz. - 17
    Emeline - 24
    Flora - 24
    Franklin - 24, 60
    Geo. - 24, 25*
    John - 25, 48, 61
    Laura - 61
    Lew Ellen - 25
    Lucy - 25
    McKinley - 38

    Margret - 25
    Mary - 24
    Mildred/Millard - 24, 25*
    Permelia - 60
    Sarah/Sally - 25, 61
    Susan/Susannah - 39, 48
    Thompson - 25
    Viola - 95
    Wm. - 25*, 48, 60

MANARD
    Joseph - 25
    Mary - 25

    Nancy - 25

MANN
    Arminda - 25
    Cilla - 113
    Didema/Demia - 25, 44, 48
    Emily Jane - 55
    Helen - 25
    James - 25
    John - 49

    Lyda - 73
    Martha/Patsy - 49*
    Martin - 49, 55
    Mary - 55
    Priscilla - 49
    Sallie - 95
    Sid - 102
    Wm. - 25

MARKHAM/MARCUM
    A. J. - 94, 108
    Albert(?) - 102
    Edwin - 25
    Elenor - 23
    Eliz. - 88

    Florence - 108
    James - 25
    Lurana - 25
    Nannie - 66
    Nellie - 94

MARSHALL
    Alfred - 80
    Anna - 9
    Benj. Franklin - 60
    Eleanor - 8
    Franklin (see Benj. F)
    Heny(?) C. - 25
    Janie - 72
    Joannah - 49

    Margaret - 25
    Mary - 56
    Nancy/Nannie - 93*, 103, 105
    Robt. - 49
    Sarah - 56, 60, 106
    Virginia - 25
    Wm. - 56, 60

MARTIN
    Elisha - 25
    Fannie - 70
    John - 70
    Kate - 70

    Nancy - 25
    Sarah - 4
    Sidney - 25

MAYS/MAISE/MAIZE/MAZE
-----? (fem) - 65, 68   Martha - 66
   Abijah - 26   Mary - 61
   Andrew - 26, 49   Merilda - 1
   Harrison - 102   Nancy - 26
   Harvey - 26, 49   Nathaniel - 26
   Henry - 26*, 49   Nestie - 69
   Hijah - 26   Nettie - 102
   Jackson - 60   Price - 102
   Jane - 62   Rachel/Racheal -
   Joanna - 26   26*, 49
   John - 102   Sarah - 63
   Lucinda/Lousinda -   Vina - 109
      71, 80   Whitley - 102
   Margaret - 60   Wm. - 26
   Marinda - 63   Zerilda - 1
MEADOWS
   Charley - 102   J. D. - 102
MEDCALF (see METCALF)
MENEFEE
   Bell - 19*
METCALF/METCALFE/MEDCALF
   Alice - 91   Joshua - 60
   Callie - 72   Louretta - 106
   James - 106
MEYERS
   W. T. - 102
MILLER
   male - 26, 49   Lettie - 102
   Arrela/Orrelia -   Louisa - 26
      26, 49   Mathias -26
   Captolia - 71   Owen - 26
   Christina - 27   Paulina/Polina -
   Elhannon - 26, 69   26*
   Florence - 26   Sarah - 96
   Geo. - 26, 102   Stephen - 26
   Ida - 26   Vina - 110
   J. E. - 102   Wm. Letcher - 26*
   Josiah - 26, 49
MILLS
   Eliz. - 5*
MINTER
   Callie - 90   Joe - 102
MONTGOMERY
   Mollie - 86

MOORE
   Arrena - 18*
   Emeline - 66
   Rebecca - 100
   Riley - 102
MOPPIN
   Ibbie - 100
MORGAN
   Lulu - 86
MORRAN
   Lola - 101
MORRIS
   Archibald - 26
   Ettie - 93
   Francis - 60
MURILL
   Matilda - 30

   Roxey - 71
   Tandy - 71
   W. J. - 71
   Wm. - 100

   J. W. - 93
   Joseph - 26
   Lucinda - 26

NAPIER
   James - 71
   Leona - 73
NEWMAN
   male - 26*
   -----? (male) - 76
   Callie - 83
   E. - 80
   Elias - 27
   Ellen - 27
   H. H. - 103
   Henry - 103
   John - 27, 80*
   Katty - 27
   Leanah/Leonia - 19*
NEWTON
   Allen - 80
   Decatur - 27
   Edna - 71
   Eliz. - 13
   Ella - 49
   Ellen - 16
   Flemmon - 71, 80
   Godfrey - 27
   Henry - 27
   Ibby/Abba - 13
   John - 27, 80
   Jordan - 27

   Mary - 71
   P. C. - 71

   Lucinda - 26*
   Lula - 110
   Margaret - 14, 56
   Martha - 13, 14
   Mary - 27, 76
   Morris - 26*
   Nancy - 27
   Robt. - 103
   S. P(?) - 103
   Sarah - 61
   Sookey - 76

   Julia - 27
   Lillie - 97
   Lucinda/Lousinda -
     71, 80
   Maggie - 107
   Martha - 27
   Mary - 27
   Nancy - 14, 27, 80
   Rachel - 27, 80
   Rauley - 49
   Richard - 27
   Wm. - 27, 49

NICHOLS
   Eliz. - 39
NOLAND/NOLEN (see also KOWLEN)
   Christina - 27   Lemuel - 49, 60
   Georgella - 27   Louis - 60
   Henry - 27   Sarah - 49
NORMAN
   Alford - 88   Maggie - 84
   Grant - 103   Mary/Mary Ann - 6
   L. C. Jr. - 103   Owen - 61
   Laura - 88

O'CONNOR
   Green - 103   Ursula Jane - 103
   Mike - 103
OLDHAM
   John - 27   Rhoda - 27
   Lewis - 27
OLINGER
   Cyntha/Cynthian -   H. B. - 71
      23, 59   Ira - 27
   Daniel - 27   Margret - 71
   Emily - 111   Phoebe - 27
   G. B. - 71
OLIVER
   Eliz. - 27*   Malvina/Malvan/
   Geo. - 27, 28, 49, 103   Malvar - 27,
   Gilford H. - 27   28, 49
   John - 27, 49   Samuel - 27*
   Luther - 27   Wm. - 28
OVERBEE
   Allice - 55
OWSLEY
   Jesse - 103

PALMER/PARMER
   Archibald - 28   John - 28, 103*
   Cordelia - 28   Link - 80*
   Delila - 64   Maggie - 85
   Dora - 85   Manda - 28
   Elender - 28   Maranda/Miranda -
   Elias - 50   28*
   Farinda - 28   Marion - 80
   Geo. - 28   Mary - 28*, 80
   Green - 28   Nancy - 15*, 21*,
   James - 28*   47*
   Jerry - 80   (cont.)

PALMER/PARMER (cont.)
  Reubin/Rubin - 28*, 80
  Varina - 28   Walker - 103
  Vina - 28
PARKER
  Selia - 87
PARSONS
  Emily - 110   Lillie - 70
  H. T(?) - 97   Phebe - 24
  J. Z(?) - 94   Zion - 104
  Josie - 110
PARTINGTON
  Ellen - 27
PATERSON
  Eliz. - 77   Thos. - 77
  Martha - 77
PAUL
  A. H. - 71   John - 71
  Capitolia - 71
PENCE
  Joab - 104   Newton - 104
PENDERGRASS
  J. - 85   Manerva - 85
  Louisa - 66
PHILLIPS
  male - 28   Harah - 107
  Adam/Adda M. - 28   Henry - 28
  B. F. - 43   Rhoda - 43
  Cleveland - 104   Silas - 61
  Eliz. - 28   Susan - 43
  Frances - 28*   Thos. - 28*
  Geo. - 104   Wm. - 28
PIGG
  Cattie - 84   Nancy - 28*
  Eveline - 28   Remus - 28
  Jackson - 28   Thomas - 28
  Mary Jane - 58
PITMAN
  female(?) - 29   Mary/Polly - 29
  Chas. - 104   Micajah - 50
  Gilly Ann - 29   Nancy - 4
  Ida - 94   Rosa - 29
  Jane - 22   Sally/Sally Ann -
  Jesse - 29, 104   20, 58
  M. C. - 104
PITT
  Almeda - 10

PLOWMAN
    Albert - 29   Sallie - 29
    Emeline - 13   Theophilus - 29
    Mollie - 111
PLUMMER
    America - 9*, 44   Mary Ann - 59
    Lucinda - 53, 59   Sarah - 5
PORTER
    John - 95   Lewis - 61
POWELL
    Bertha - 84   Minerva - 50
    J. D. - 104   Monroe - 50
    John - 50
PRICE (see PRYSE)
PRICHARD/PRITCHARD
    Annie - 29   John - 105
    Eliz. - 29   Joseph - 29
    Jilson - 29   Rutha - 29
PROFITT/PROFFITT
    Anna - 107   James - 29*
    Christney -107   Jesse - 29
    Dulcena - 63   Lucinda - 63
    Eli - 29   Mary - 29*
    Elijah - 29   Patience - 29*
    Eliz. - 29*   Sena - 37, 63
    H. F. - 105   Wilgus - 29
    Ira - 29   Wm. - 29
PRYSE/PRICE
    -----? (fem) - 71*   Moses - 71*
    Brack - 104   Nannie - 50
    David - 29, 50   S. E. (fem) - 80
    Elias - 29   Sallie Ann - 71
    Eliz. - 29   Stanley - 71
    John - 104   Thos. - 80, 104
    Louellen(?) - 80   Viola - 29
    Lucy - 29, 50   W. C. - 71
    Mary - 71   Zacheriah - 29
    Mattie(?) - 71
PUCKETT
    Barthena - 92   Sally - 39

QUILLEN
    Chas. - 30   Harlan - 30, 105
    Delina - 30
QUINTER
    Grace - 112   W. H. - 112

QUINTON
    Oliver - 105

RADER/RAIDER
    Albert - 105   Joseph - 105
    John - 105   Mary - 16*
RAGAN
    Rebecca - 36
RANKINS
    Nannie - 88
RASNER
    Mary/Polly - 80   Wm. - 80
    Noah - 80
RATLIFF
    Ara - 91
REED/READ
    Amanda - 31   Matilda - 30
    Enoch - 30   Rebecca - 30
    Geo. - 30   Shelton - 30
    Jane - 30   Weber - 30
    John - 30   Willie (fem) - 68
    Mary - 30
REESE
    Elijah - 30*   Judah - 61
    Francis - 30   Lucian - 105
    John - 61   Sarah/Sally - 30*
    Joseph - 61   Zerilda - 30
REYNOLDS
    Mary - 13
RHODES
    Permelia - 60
RICHARDSON
    Delila - 93   Nannie - 68
    Len(?) - 105   Sarah/Sally - 30*
RILEY
    Dan - 89   Mertie - 71
    Eva - 89   Nancy - 30
    James - 30   R. B. - 71
    John - 105   Sallie - 2
    May - 71   Zachary - 30
ROACH
    Amanda - 80   Geo. - 30, 106
    Ance/Anderson - 30*   John - 30
    Armina - 16*   Liddia - 80
    Bertha - 104   Margaret - 30
    Cath. - 30   R. (fem) - 80
    Eliz/Lizzie - 94   (cont.)

152

ROACH (cont.)
    Rebecca - 30
    Sylvester - 30
ROBERTS
    America - 39*
    Eda - 32
    Eliz. - 50
    Helen - 25
    James - 50
    John - 50
    Logan - 106
ROBINSON/ROBERTSON
    John - 50*
    Josephine - 14
    Mahaley - 35
    Mary Etta - 101
    Matilda - 11
ROGERS/RODGERS
    Amanda - 31
    Charley - 106
    Eliza - 9, 43
    Isaac - 31
ROLLEN (see ROWLAND)
ROSE
    America - 6
    Asa - 106
    Paulina/Polina - 26*
ROSS
    female - 31
    Amanda - 76
    Cassie - 71
    Castora - 50
    Delina - 31, 76
    Emily - 31
    Geo. - 71
    Grant - 72
    Green B. - 106
    Henry - 31, 76
ROWE
    Clint - 106
ROWLAND/ROLLEN
    Ida - 80
    Nannie - 83

SALYER
    Maud - 67*, 77

Thos. - 30*, 80
Wm. - 30

Lucinda - 30, 48
Lurinda - 59
Mary/Polly - 32, 51
Moses - 30*
Nancy - 30*
Susan - 58

Nancy - 25
Omega - 109
Rhoda - 50
Widow(?) - 101
Wm. - 109

John -61
Mattie - 31
Roxsie - 83

Rosa - 73

Herrod - 50*
James - 50
Larry - 50
Martha - 43, 50, 72
Millard - 31
Nettie - 71
Peter - 50
Robt. - 72
Tabitha - 32
Vina - 50*

Thos. - 106

153

SAMS
    Emily - 81
    Helm(?) - 81
    J. M. - 106
    Wm. - 81
SAMPLES
    Emily - 102
    Sarah - 102
SAMPLES/STAMPER(?)
    Jackson - 81
    Jesse - 81
    Nancy - 81
SCHOLL (see also SHULL)
    Ella - 31
    Larry(?) Lee - 31
    Laura - 50
    Lawrence - 50
    Wm. - 31, 50
SEALE
    Leah - 81
    Martha - 96
SEWELL
    Fanny/Fannie - 3*
    Mack - 111
SHACK
    Nannie - 110
SHACKELFORD
    Addie May - 111
    Eliz. - 27, 28*
    Elsie - 72
    James - 31
    Louisa - 26
    Mandrel - 31*
    Mariam - 31*
    Mary Ann - 31
    S. B. - 72
    Santford - 31
    Sarah - 72
SHAFFER
    Clarence - 106
SHANKS
    Fanny - 106
    Tilman - 106, 110
SHEARER
    Albert - 61
    Alice - 39*, 63
    Geo. - 61
    Lucien - 106
    Mary - 2
    Narcissa - 61
SHEPARD
    Barbara - 38
    Emmon - 31, 61
    Franklin - 31
    Rebecca - 31
SHOEMAKER
    Andrew - 31*, 32
    Cordie - 72
    Daniel - 31
    Elisha - 61
    Eliz. - 54
    Enos(?) - 107
    Eullar/Uller - 31
    Evaline/Eveline/
        Evoline 31*, 32, 72
    Flora - 74
    Henna(?) - 31
    Henry - 31, 61, 72
    Hiram - 107
    Jane - 36*, 52
    John - 91
    Luther - 72
    Margt.(see Evaline)
    Mertie - 72
    Millard/Millades 31
        (cont.)

154

SHOEMAKER (cont.)
  Sabra - 31
  Sarah - 19*, 46
  Susannah - 61
SHORT
  Asa - 107
SHOUSE
  Betie - 107
SHULL/SCHULL (see also SCHOLL)
  Lillie - 104
SIMS
  Elisa - 97
SIMMS(?)
  J. R - 107
SIZEMORE
  Zilla - 85
SLONE/SLOAN
  male - 51
  Bethena - 56
  Clem - 107
  Eliza - 58
  Jesse - 58
  Juda - 47
  Lucinda - 58
  Mary - 32
SMALLWOOD
  Annie - 81
  David E. - 32, 51
  Edmund (see David E.)
  Elias - 51
  Eliz. - 32
  John - 32, 81
  Louania - 32
SMITH/SMYTH
  male - 32, 51, 72
  Abraham - 32*
  Ada - 88
  Alice - 94, 99
  Asa - 32
  B. - 99
  Benj. - 72
  Breckinridge - 62
  Brenis(?) - 72
  C. B. - 72
  Callie - 72, 87
  Caroline - 32*
  Chas/Charley - 32, 107

Thos. - 31, 72
Wm. - 31, 107
Woodford - 32

Mollie - 74

Wrenna - 90

John - 107

Nancy - 25
Nathan - 51
Rolla - 107
Sarilda/Zerilda
  - 32*
Shadric - 62
Susan - 51
Wm. - 32*

Lucy - 32, 51, 112
Margaret - 52
Martha - 81
Mary - 27
Rachel - 52
Randall - 52
Rosilla - 32

Clay - 32
Daniel - 72
Dudly - 107
Eda - 32
Edna - 72
Effie - 83
Eliz./Bettie - 72
  111
Ellen - 91
Ellie Green - 89
Emeline - 8
Emmitt - 107
  (cont.)

SMITH/SMYTH (cont.)
    Enoch - 107
    Felix - 32
    G. B. - 72
    Geo. - 32*, 83, 89
    Henry - 32*, 51, 54
    Hiram U.S. Grant - 32
    Hugh - 51
    Huram - 32, 87
    Isaac - 32
    J. P. - 111
    James - 32
    Jane/Janie - 18, 54,
        72, 76
    John - 32*, 33, 62*
        72, 108
    Julia - 32
    Kaner - 76
    Keen - 33
    L. E. - 72
    Lella - 105
    Loratte - 107
    Lou - 81*
    Louisa - 54
    Louvina - 10*
SNODGRASS
    America - 7
SNOWDEN
    Alex. - 33
    Clarinda - 49, 60
    Dora - 33
    Enos - 33, 108
    Francis M. - 33, 49,
        60
    James - 62
    John - 33*, 62
    Laura - 81
SPARKS
    Elisha - 51
    Eliz. - 9, 33
    Henry - 33
    Isaac - 51
    Joseph - 33
    Kate - 70
    Martha - 65
    Nancy/Nannie - 33, 86

    Lucinda - 51
    Lucy - 32*, 72
    Margaret 21, 48, 76
    Martha - 110
    Mary/Polly - 32*,
        51, 54
    Matt - 108
    May - 99
    Milton - 98, 108
    Nancy - 28*
    Nettie - 101
    Ollie - 87
    Orfa - 22
    Rachel - 39
    Rebecca - 64
    Robt. - 108
    Routh(?) - 81
    Sarah/Sally -
        14, 72
    Shirley - 72
    Sophia - 32
    Taulby - 108
    Wiley - 51
    Wm. - 81

    Armina - 7

    Letcher - 81
    Lucy - 62
    Lydia/Lidia - 33*
    Margret - 62
    Mary/Polly - 33
    Paulina - 62
    Russel - 81
    Sarah - 49

    Ollie - 108
    Samuel - 108
    Sarah/Sallie - 29,
        94
    Sylvester - 33
    Thos. - 33

SPENCE
    Frank - 108   Henry - 108
SPENCER
    Adda - 87   John - 51
    Amanda - 12*   Lucinda - 26, 67
    Anna - 4   Margaret - 33*, 34
    Cath. - 51   Martha - 51
    Deborah - 33   Mary - 29, 33*, 49
    Edy - 33   Matilda - 9
    Ella - 33   Moses - 33
    Eulia - 33   Nancy - 54
    Geo. W. - 33*   Nicholas - 33*
    Isaac - 49   S. - 87
    Isaiah - 33   Sanford - 33
    Isham - 33   Sarah - 20*, 92, 93
    Jesse - 33   Simeon - 34
    Joannah - 49   Wm. - 33, 34
SPICER
    female - 72   Mettie - 92
    -----? (fem) - 72   Millie - 112
    Berry - 108   Ned - 92
    Eliza - 34   Samuel - 34, 81
    Ellis - 81   Sarah/Sallie - 89,
    Evaline - 35   92
    Grandville - 62   Wm. - 72
    Mary/Polly - 34
SPIVY/SPIVEY/SPIVA (see also SPRAY)
    Geo. - 97, 105   Martha - 5
    Laura - 97
SPRAY (see also SPIVY)
    Mattie - 105
SPUR
    Phillip - 46
STACY
    Alba - 34   Martin - 34
    Annie - 87   Melvina - 34*
    Breck - 108   Nettie - 87
    Genilla/Geniva - 34   Rosa - 34
    Laura - 86   Wm. - 34*
    Mart - 86   Zarilda - 34
STAFFORD
    Hariet - 23   Willie - 109
STAMPER
    female - 72   Amanda/Amandy - 68,
    -----? (fem) - 111   77*
    Ada/Edda - 34, 35   Arminta - 2*
    Albert - 63   (cont.)

157

STAMPER (cont.)
    Burton - 109
    Callie - 109
    Cath. - 72*
    Cynthia - 34
    Dora - 34
    E. J. - 72*
    Earley - 34
    Edward - 34, 35, 77
    Eliza - 34
    Eliz/Lizzie - 34, 100
    Ellis - 81
    Emanuel - 109
    Emily - 59, 100
    Enoch - 109
    Flored - 73
    Florence - 34
    Floyd - 34
    Frankie - 113
    Geo. W. - 34
    Gilly Ann - 38
    Grover - 109
    Huston - 109
    J. A. - 100
    Jackson - 81
    James - 34
    Jane - 62
    Jesse - 81
    Joel - 34, 35, 51
    John - 34*, 58
    Joseph - 34, 109
STEEL/STEELE
    Carlee Bayde - 73
    Daniel - 35
    Elmer - 73
    Emma - 73
    Florence/Flawrence
        - 73, 81
    J. W. - 109
    John - 81
    Margret - 35
STEPHENS
    Anna - 6
    Bert - 109
    STEPP
    Mary - 103

    Judith - 34
    Larkin - 51
    Lewis - 62, 81
    Loueller - 34
    Lucinda - 58
    Lula - 67
    Martha - 104, 109
    Mary/Polly - 33, 34
        35, 51, 57, 109
    Matilda/Tildy - 34,
        35, 42, 57, 77
    Millard - 34, 35
    Millie - 81
    Minetree - 72
    Nancy - 63, 81
    Pearl - 73
    Peter - 62, 109
    Phebe Jane - 18, 58
    Samuel - 35
    Sarah/Sally/Sallie
        - 34, 35, 63,
        72*, 73, 107
    Sophia - 103
    Susan - 35
    Sylvana - 34
    W. C. - 109
    W. O. B. - 109
    Wm. - 34

    Martha/Patsy -
        35, 36
    Mary/Polly - 35
    Nannie - 7, 55
    Rebeca - 1
    Stonewall - 73
    Thos. - 35, 73
    Wm. - 35

    Martha - 89

STERNBERG
    Alice - 87   Mahaley - 35
    Felix - 35   Saml. - 35
STIDHAM
    Andrew - 109   Nancy - 109
    James - 109
STONE
    Bettie - 73   Rollen - 73
    Melvina - 34*   Rosa - 73
STRANBURY
    Geo. - 110
STRANGE
    Margaret - 37
STRONG
    A. J. - 110   Maggie - 73
    Alex. - 35*, 51   Mary - 51
    Andrew/Andy - 35, 73   Mattie - 90
    Elijah - 73   Nancy - 35
    Evaline - 35   Rosa - 73
    Georgie - 84   Sarah/Sallie - 35,
    James - 62   51, 73, 90
    Lillie - 73   Thos. - 35
    Lydia - 35
SULLIVAN/SULAVAN
    Golden - 73   Sarah - 73
    Mary - 38   Thos. - 73
SUTTON
    Kathalene - 107   May - 90
SWAN
    John - 110
SWEENEY
    Curt - 110

TAYLOR
    Albert - 81   Maranda - 109
    Jane (male) - 81   Nancy - 81
TEWART
    James - 35   Mary/Polly - 35*
    Lucy - 35   Robt. - 35*
THACKER
    Elisha - 110   Martha - 36
    James - 36   Sallie - 36
THARPE/THARP
    Ellen - 69   Oliver - 36
    Jesse - 36   Rebecca - 36

THOMAS
    -----? (male) - 82
    A. F. - 73
    Aaron/Aron - 73
    Anthony - 62
    Cath. - 36
    Cora - 73
    David Sale - 52
    Diadema- 52
    Eleanor Cath. - 51
    Eliz. - 62, 82*
    Emma - 36
    Eva - 111
    Garfield - 110
    Geo. - 62
    Henry - 36*, 52, 82
    James - 36, 51, 53,
       62, 82, 110
    Jane - 36*, 52*, 82
    Jesse - 52*
    John - 102
    Joseph - 36, 62

    Leona - 73
    Lizzie - 73
    Lucy - 62
    Margarett/Margret -
       24, 58, 79
    Martha - 36
    Mary - 2*, 5, 17,
       53*, 82
    Millard - 73
    Nancy - 5
    Paulina - 62
    Price - 73
    S. P. - 82
    Samuel - 110
    Sarah - 17, 46, 91
    Stella - 36
    Susan- 36
    Varr - 52
    W. G. - 73
    Wm. - 36, 73, 82
    Zachariah - 52

THOMPSON
    Cath. - 36
    Eleanor Cath. - 36,
      51, 62
    Lydia/Lidia - 33*, 62
    Lottie - 100
    Louisa - 100
    Mary/Polly - 33, 51, 62

    Nancy - 36
    Sarah - 36, 56, 60
    Sylvanus - 63
    Wm. - 36, 51, 62
    Winnie - 22

TINCHER
    Albert - 36
    Asa - 36*, 82
    Elisha - 82
    Eliza - 19, 47
    Esther - 49
    Felix - 36
    Henry Etta - 36
    James - 36, 58
    Lucy Ann - 17*, 58
    Margaret/Margret -
      7, 52, 108, 112
    Martha/Patsy - 49*, 82

    Nancy - 36
    Nora - 108
    Priscilla - 49
    Randall/Randolf 36*
    Rebecca - 36
    Samuel - 49
    Sarah - 36*
    Susannah/Susanah -
      36, 58
    W. H. - 110
    Wm. - 36, 52

TIPTON/TYPTON
    Chas. - 111
    Ellie(?) - 70
    Gincey - 93

    Lula - 99
    Mary - 20, 47, 94
    Millard - 110

TOLBY
    Alwilda - 48   Judith - 34
    Anna - 22   Sarah - 22
TOLER
    Ella - 93   Mary Belle - 94
    J. W. - 73   Ollie - 73
    Joseph - 73   Polina - 112
    Lillie - 89   Rose - 73
    Logan - 110   Willis - 73
    Lyda - 73
TOMLINSON
    Hanah - 16
TOWNSEND
    female - 37   John - 111
    Ada/Edda - 34, 35   Margaret - 37
    Eliz. - 62   Nancy - 55
    Fannie - 63   Rus (fem) - 37
    Geo. - 37, 63   Sarah(?) - 37
    James - 37   Sena - 37
    Jerry - 37
TREADWAY
    Arch - 111   Helen - 24*
    Bascom - 111   Mary Frances - 37
    Demia - 63   Sam - 111
    Frances - 37   Thos. - 63
    Geo. - 37   Wm. - 37*, 63
    Getha - 85
TRENT
    Ben - 111
TRIMBLE
    Cynthia - 21, 59   Evaline - 42
TROUSE
    Phoebe - 27
TURLEY
    Mary - 40, 64   Rebecca - 64
    Michael - 64
TURNER
    male - 74   Matilda/Tildy -
    ----? (male) 111*   34*, 77
    Amanda - 82   Millie - 81
    Cager - 74   Mollie - 74
    D. - 111   Nancy - 74, 91
    D. G. - 74   R. L. - 99
    David - 63   Richard - 82
    Hellen - 74   Sarah - 2
    John - 111   Silas - 111
    Mary/Mary Ann - 62, 99

161

TURPIN
    Sally May - 112
TURRELL
    Joseph - 111
TWYMAN
    Broaddus - 37*   Lucy - 37*
    Leslie - 37   Sidney - 37
TYLER
    male - 37   Mary 37
    Chas. - 37
TYPTON (see TIPTON)
TYRA/TYRE/TYREE/TIREY
    C. G. - 112   Joannah - 59
    Carrey - 97   Sarah - 105

UNDERWOOD
    Lou - 88
UPTHEGROVE(?)
    Olia - 112

VANDERPOOL
    female(?) - 37*   George Ella - 38
    male - 37   Ibzan - 38
    Abraham - 37   Isaac - 37*, 38*
    Amanda - 37*   Jacob -63
    America - 37   Paulina - 38
    Delitha - 37, 38   Rachel/Racheal -
    E. D. - 112   37*, 38*
    Elbert - 38   Therisa - 38
    Eliz. - 8*   Udocia - 38
    Enoch - 37, 38   Wm. - 38*
VAUGHN
    Polly - 97
VIRES
    Barthena - 82

WADE
    Cely - 52   Millard - 112
    Hiram - 52   Wm. - 112
    Ira - 52
WALTON
    Amanda - 13   Mariah - 109
    Geo. - 109
WARD
    Charley - 112   Mary - 38
    Geo. W. - 38   Ota - 38
    Maggie - 18

162

WARNER
   Evaline/Evoline -   Jeff - 112
      13, 56   Wm. - 63
WARREN
   Mary - 3
WARWICK
   Wm. - 112
WATKINS
   Sallie - 84
WATSON
   Boone D. - 38   Rebecca - 38*, 82
   Daniel Boone - 38   Wm. - 38
   Manda - 38
WATTS
   Joanna - 26
WEAR
   Andele - 112
WEBB
   James - 38   Martha - 38 *
   Josiah - 38*   Mervin - 38
   Manda - 28   Nettie - 71
WEILER
   Margret - 57
WELLS
   Hettiller(?) - 52   Mary - 52
   Israel - 63   Rebecca - 13
   John - 52   Wm. - 63
   Martha - 8
WHEELER
   Nettie - 101
WHISMAN
   Barbara - 38   Moses - 38
   Enoch - 38   Nancy - 66
   Gilly Ann - 38   Rosanah - 38
   Job - 38
WHITE
   America - 39*   James - 39*
   Aquilla - 42   Lottie - 102
   Arzella - 107   Martha/Patsy - 42,
   B. F. - 56   55
   Drucilla - 39   Melissa - 22
   Emily - 56   Netie(?) - 74
   Franklin (see B. F.) Oda - 114
   Fred - 39   P. D. - 74
   Grant - 102   Sally - 42, 56
   Harland - 74

WILLIAMS
    A. - 61
    Alice - 39*
    Andrew - 39
    Clark - 74
    Cleveland - 112
    Delila - 106
    Edgar - 39
    Elijah - 112
    Eliza - 39
    Ethel - 74
    Everine - 52
    Flora - 74
    Frederic - 39
    Geo. - 52*

    H. - 106
    Hasiah - 61
    Henna(?) - 31
    John - 39*, 63
    Joseph - 113
    Lora/Lory - 39, 69
    Lucy - 32*, 62
    Mahala/Mahaley/Haley
      - 22, 59
    Million - 39
    Nancy - 62
    Noah - 39
    Sally - 39, 61

WILLIEN
    Henson - 113
WILLIS
    Eliz. - 16
    Emeline - 24

    Mary - 60

WILOBY
    Craxton - 113
WILSON/WILLSON
    A. - 53
    Alice - 39
    Barnie - 113
    Berlie - 74
    David - 39, 64, 74
    Eliz. - 9
    Florence - 102

    Hannah - 2*, 41, 53
    Laura - 90
    Mary - 39, 53, 74
    Mertie - 72
    Mint(?) - 89, 98
    Rellie - 113

WINKLE
    Almeda/Amelia - 5*

    Eliz. - 28

WIRES
    Bailey - 113
WITT
    Price - 113
WOOD
    Cath. - 30
WOODEN
    Geo. - 39

    Thos. - 39

    Rachel - 39
WOOSLEY
    James - 113
WREGL(?)
    Lewis - 93

WRIGHT
    male - 39*
    Charlottie - 21
    Claude - 39, 52
    Eliz. - 39
    James - 113
    Lewis - 39
    Louisa/Loula/Lucella/
       Louella/Luella -
       39*, 40*, 52
    Marshall - 39

Martha - 39
Maud - 40
Phoebe/Pheba - 10,
   11, 44
Robt. - 40
Sarah - 55
Susan - 16, 39
Thos. - 39*, 40*,
   52

WYATT
    Deller - 40
    Geo. - 40, 64

Mary - 10, 27, 40
Wm. - 64

YORK
    Alfred - 40
    Ellen - 40*
    John - 40

Robt. - 113
Wm. - 40*

YOUNG
    Dave - 111
    Henry - 64

Martha - 111
Samuel - 114

www.ingramcontent.com/pod-product-compliance
Lightning Source LLC
Chambersburg PA
CBHW070839300326
41935CB00038B/1151